Nearly Famous

Secrets, Lies and Videotape

REBA MERRILL
with Ginny Weissman

Foreword by
Dee Wallace

Introduction by
Pete Hammond

Open Books
PRESS

Published by Open Books Press, USA
www.openbookspress.com

An imprint of Pen & Publish, Inc.
Bloomington, Indiana
(812) 837-9226
info@PenandPublish.com

www.PenandPublish.com

Copyright © 2012 Reba Merrill

Cover photo by Richard Hiltzik
All rights reserved.
No part of this book may be reproduced, stored in a retrieval system, or transmitted
by any means, electronic, mechanical, photocopying, recording, or otherwise,
except for brief passages in connection with a review,
without written permission from the author.

ISBN: 978-0-9852737-6-7
Library of Congress Number: 2012937288

This book is printed on acid free paper.

Printed in the USA

"*Nearly Famous* is nearly like sitting across a table from the world's biggest stars and sharing a cup of coffee. Reba finds the humanity in even the larger than life personalities and splashes it across the page. A must read for movie fans everywhere."

Mark DeCarlo
TV host and author
A Fork on the Road: 400 Cities, One Stomach

"A unique insider's look behind the scenes and into the star's lives—all before TMZ and celebrity television. Reba lifted the veil on the making of ---the making of."

Stuart Samuels
Producer/Director
Visions of Light; *Midnight Movies*; *Hollywoodism*

"I thoroughly enjoyed reading the book and was impressed how Reba kept reinventing herself. She filled a void in film promotion that the rest of us weren't even aware existed and gave us important new ways of presenting our movies to the film-going public."

Patricia Kingsley
Former chairman-CEO of PMK/HBH

"Reading Reba's remarkable story of how she found her groove in this business you come to realize the makings of a real pro…a highly entertaining memoir and, as usual, pulls no punches. Read it. Enjoy it. Be seduced by it."

Pete Hammond
Writer, Producer, Movie Critic and Film Historian

"Not just a wonderful romp through Hollywood's A-List stars, *Nearly Famous: Secrets, Lies, and Videotape* also is an honest and open look at ageism in the entertainment industry and the misery of sugar addiction. Highly, highly recommended reading."

Winona Phillabaum
Manager of The Lloyd Taber Library, Marina del Rey, CA

*It is not because things are difficult that we
do not dare;
it is because we do not dare that they are difficult.*
$\sim$ Seneca

Dedication

To Jan, my wonderful husband. I was madly in love with him when we first met. I never thought it could be possible, but I love him even more today.

To my children, who grew up with an unconventional mother and made it anyway.

Contents

Foreword by Dee Wallace	ix
Introduction by Pete Hammond	xi
Preface	xiii
Chapter One	1
Chapter Two	11
Chapter Three	17
Chapter Four	25
Chapter Five	31
Chapter Six	35
Chapter Seven	41
Chapter Eight	49
Chapter Nine	57
Chapter Ten	65
Chapter Eleven	71
Chapter Twelve	75
Chapter Thirteen	79
Chapter Fourteen	85
Chapter Fifteen	91
Chapter Sixteen	97
Chapter Seventeen	101
Chapter Eighteen	105
Chapter Nineteen	109
Chapter Twenty	115
Chapter Twenty-one	119
Chapter Twenty-two	123
Chapter Twenty-three	127
Chapter Twenty-four	131
Epilogue	133
Acknowledgments	135
Celebrity List	137
About the Author	143
About the Collaborator	145

Foreword

I have known Reba for over twenty years, and yet I feel I haven't really known her at all after reading *Nearly Famous: Secrets, Lies and Videotape*. I knew Reba as a kind, professional journalist who helped enhance my career with an amazing interview she did with me for the film *Cujo*, after the opening of *E.T.* Over the next years, our paths would cross at charity events and various Hollywood functions, and there was always an unspoken bond of friendship I could never quite put my finger on. Not the kind of friendship where you "do lunch" and meet for drinks. This was the kind of friendship that, although mostly unspoken, existed in a kind of "knowing" about life and what was real.

Little did I know, it was the beginning of her career, also.

I would come to find out that my trust and participation was her jump into the big time, and that made us reciprocal souls in the journey of destiny making. Both of us started in humble beginnings. Both of us valued integrity. Both of us had the good old American work ethic implanted in us at an early age. And most importantly, both of us had the highest valued aspect for success: naiveté and belief in ourselves.

We didn't care if it was hard, or too challenging, or improbable. There was a force within us that discounted the naysayers and whispered, "Go do your dream anyway."

So join Reba in her fascinating journey of being a rather small town girl, making it in Hollywood and interviewing some of the biggest names in cinematic history. It is a tribute to that part in all of us that had a dream and still does. Take a journey and peek into the person that helps shape the information and glimpses of the people you read about, and how they protect us—and expose us—for you.

Our careers, and lives, can be changed forever by the pictures of us they paint for you. Reba, fortunately, was one of those powerful people driven by love and integrity. I am honored to have been the first.

Dee Wallace
March 12, 2012

Dee Wallace has worked as an author, teacher, dancer and actress in film, television and the stage for over 30 years. With over 100 credits to her name, Ms. Wallace is perhaps best known for her roles in several popular films. These include a starring role as Elliot's mother in the Steven Spielberg film *E.T. the Extra-Terrestrial* (1982). She also played key roles in popular cult films *The Hills Have Eyes* (1977), *The Howling* (1981) and *Cujo* (1983). www.iamdeewallace.com

Introduction

I can remember the first moment I met Reba Merrill. She had a certain style and manner you don't often encounter in this business, a seductiveness that was purely business but totally enchanting.

Reba made me feel like I was the most important person in the world, at least at that moment. Again, I will use the word seductive. I was working as a producer at Entertainment Tonight and she was doing electronic press kits for studios or EPKs as they are known. Usually this kind of homogenized canned movie star interview was handed off to me by studio publicists. Generally I ignored the interview portions because they were so promotional in nature I could hardly make compelling television out of them. Anyway we did our OWN interviews. But not always. The rare exception was almost always a Reba interview.

There was something uniquely different about her work. It actually was watchable. Unlike most of these studio-sanctioned interviews she managed to cut to the chase and get to the heart of her interview subjects whether it was a big star or some third level supporting player. I am still not sure how she did it, but I think I developed some of my own interviewing style just watching her stuff on those tapes. She had the knack, but I was surprised she ever got hired to do these because the material was so NOT what I had come to expect from these manufactured interview packages. Reba knew how to sell a movie precisely by not selling it and she got remarkable insights from all those many stars, some of them certifiable legends. Somehow she used those seductive powers to get what she wanted and you could just tell that after a long day of press they were glad to see her.

Reading her remarkable story of how she found her groove in this business you come to realize the makings of a real pro. She suffered the slings and arrows of what was expected, all those years in local TV, struggling to get ahead, to find her path, her rhythm and her self-esteem. It wasn't easy. And it clearly was tough navigating the shark-infested waters of show business—but she did it. And continues to do it in her own inimitable Reba-style.

And now she's written this highly entertaining memoir and, as usual, pulls no punches. Read it. Enjoy it. Be seduced by it.

Pete Hammond
March 28, 2012

Pete Hammond is a writer, producer, movie critic and film historian. His analysis and commentary on the entertainment industry has appeared in print, on air and online for numerous publications including The New York Times, Los Angeles Times, USA Today, Entertainment Weekly, New York Magazine, OK Magazine, NBC Nightly News with Tom Brokaw, Evening News with Brian Williams on MSNBC, the CBC, BBC, Bravo, E!, and AMC

Preface

Before you start reading this book, I think you should know how I began this journey. I was born in Baltimore and, like the majority of women in my generation, I was raised to be a wife and mother. Although I had appeared in many of the school plays, I didn't think I could act or sing or dance well enough to be a professional so escaping to New York to be a star was just a dream. My mother was terrified that I would run off for a career on the stage and never have what she considered to be a proper life. Instead she encouraged me to accept a marriage proposal from the strikingly handsome son of a prominent oil family in Denver who I had just met earlier that year. At seventeen, only three weeks after graduating from high school, I started my new life--not on the Broadway stage but as a socialite wife and eventually a mother. My mother's wish had come true.

Fast forward eight years and two little girls later: I am divorced (rare at the time) and faced with providing for myself and young daughters with no support from my ex-husband or his family who cut us out of their lives. Looking back, it was the best thing that could have happened to me. I got a job in public relations for a glass company in Denver and met a wonderful man, Jan Wlodarkiewicz, who would become my husband. How lucky I was to meet a man totally opposite from the one I divorced and much different from my usual "type." Jan was born in Europe, and educated at Dartmouth and Johns Hopkins School of International Relations. He treated me differently from any man I had ever dated. Jan was charming, continental and everything I ever wanted—good in bed, had a good job as a computer expert and adored my two daughters. A new safe chapter in my life began that continues to this day.

Jan pushed me to go to college, so wherever we lived around the world (including London) I went to school. At the same time, I appeared in commercials so I could make my own money to buy presents for my family. When we moved to a new city because of my husband's career, I would get a job doing commercials, except when we lived in London. There I was hired to do voiceovers because I sounded like an American. I had no thought at that point of a full-time career, nor could I even dream of living the exciting life that was about to begin.

Chapter One

I'm not a writer. I am a talker. If I hadn't been able to talk and talk and talk, I would never have had a career in the entertainment industry. Of the thousands working in Hollywood, only a handful will be famous. I sure wasn't one of them, but I was near those who were. I would never have been able to figure out how to survive the hills and valleys, of the mountains of life if I hadn't pursued a career in Hollywood. I have kept secrets and told lies, not just to others but also to myself. I admit I sometimes chose my career of interviewing celebrities on videotape over my family and struggled with a food addiction that controlled my life.

It all started when we moved to Phoenix, Arizona. I have to be honest. I really hated it. I didn't like the weather or the house, but my family was happy. Before we moved from Denver, we had a son, Mark, and Jan adopted my two daughters. Jan's love and affection for the girls gave people the impression that he was their birth father and that I was the one who had adopted them. My three children loved being in school and my husband loved his job, so I was the only one who was miserable.

When I was thirty-seven years old, I appeared in a commercial and hated it. Even though I had appeared in other commercials, I thought saying the words for that particular product made me sound stupid. I came home and announced to my family that instead of doing commercials, I would get a talk show. After the laughter subsided, I had to figure out how to actually do it. I looked up Phoenix television stations in the phonebook; there were only five at that time. Before I started on this adventure—and I have never told this to anyone—I created a "vision board," pictures of the things I wanted to happen to me. I cut out the call letters of the five Phoenix TV stations from TV Guide, and then out of other magazines, I cut five TV sets. On each screen, I placed a picture of myself. Then I called all five stations and got appointments with executives at each one. But after my meetings, everybody turned me down. I had a perfect record!

Reba Merrill

The person who interviewed me at one station told me I had to learn how to type. At another station, the executive said, "How do I know you know how to interview?"

The first time I had any hope of getting a job in television was when I met Burton LaDow, the general manager at Channel 3, then the ABC affiliate in Phoenix. He said, "not yet," a powerful response that gave me hope because I knew what "yet" meant: the difference between yes and no. All I had to do was get rid of that "t" in yet and I had a "YES."

I knew what I wanted to do, but I didn't know how to do it. If I was going to interview people, then I had better get busy learning how. I borrowed a tape recorder and convinced somebody to let me interview them. I don't even remember who it was; I only know that it worked. As I found one person, they would refer me to another, so I went around interviewing people I didn't know. It got to the point where I was really enjoying it. I wasn't nervous and I was actually having fun, but there were other things I needed to learn to be an interviewer on TV. Up until then, I had spent many years appearing in commercials in other cities so being on camera didn't frighten me.

After talking to all the television stations, I knew the first thing I had to do was to make a name for myself. When I was living in London, none of my neighbors, who happened to be very well off, bought cosmetics like we Americans do. They all gave me recipes for home-made skin care for my skin and body without buying a lot of expensive products.

I took all that information and put together a program called "Here's Egg on Your Face." At the time I was just building a name for myself — today that's called branding. I owe my branding to two wonderful women: Ellie Schultz, who was the fashion editor of the *Arizona Republic*, the major paper in Phoenix, and Pat McElfresh at the *Scottsdale Daily Progress*. I called Ellie and we just hit it off. She decided to do a major article about the "beauty expert" – me – who had moved to the Valley of the Sun. By the way, that's what they call Phoenix.

Every time I booked a speech, she would write another article about me, which generated a little more interest in my program and in me. I would use the articles to book myself into country clubs and conventions. The first speech I did was at the Paradise Valley Country Club, which was right down the street from where we lived. I dressed to the nines. I wore my designer clothes from London, including an exquisite hat. I ended the program by making a facial and literally putting egg on my face.

During these presentations people would stop me and ask: "Now, how much oatmeal did you put in that mask?" or "How ripe does the avocado have to be?" or "How much baby oil do you use in the bath?" I thought to myself this is not going to work because my talk was really a standup routine and, when they asked me questions in the middle, it broke the rhythm. I went to Lynn Castleberry, an artist who was married to my husband's boss, and I asked her if she would help me create a booklet. I tested every single recipe and wrote each of them up. My favorite was how to steam your face by opening the dishwasher during the last cycle. I didn't say I was brilliant— I just found all these ways to care for your skin in the kitchen! Lynn drew little pictures, and I put in all the recipes and had them printed in a brochure called "Here's Egg On Your Face." The next time I gave a speech, I sold the booklet for a dollar, and I came home with a fistful of dollars.

Reba Merrill

Since a lot of my speeches were in Scottsdale, Pat McElfresh at the local paper started doing articles on my booklet and on me. I would go back to Ellie Schultz and tell her what I was doing, she would write another article for the *Arizona Republic*, and I would use that to get another meeting at the television stations. I really wasn't getting any encouragement from station executives, except from Channel 3, the ABC station. I knew that I could never get in at the local NBC station because they already had a woman on the air. The one independent station had just hired a woman who could cook and sew. The man I spoke to at PBS asked me how could I do a television show if I didn't have a format. I replied, "What's a format?" He explained that typically, you have an opening, a middle, and a close, and in between those set sections you have to build segments about whom you want to interview, how long the interviews are, and the theme of the show.

I wanted to do a half-hour show and interview two or three people. I wasn't going to bite off more than I could chew. For a year I had collected information on famous people who came to Phoenix. I cut out articles from the Scottsdale and the Phoenix newspapers dreaming that these were the people I would really like to interview on my television show. When I was told that I had to come up with a format – and I will never forget this – I hauled out an orange plastic laundry bag with handles containing all these newspaper clippings, sat on the floor of our bedroom and dumped them all around me. I felt like a pioneer, and these were the covered wagons surrounding and protecting me. I started to pick out the people I really wanted to interview, if I could. I wrote a format by hand because my typing skills were non-existent and I didn't have access to a typewriter. I gave the handwritten script to my husband and asked if he would please have his secretary type up my format and make some copies.

I went back to the independent station, which had just hired a woman, to do a television show. The woman was like Sue Ann Nivens, the character Betty White played on *The Mary Tyler Moore Show*. She cooked and sewed and was very domestic, all skills that eluded me. I could cook, but I wasn't a great cook. I didn't know how to sew, except maybe a button. Being nearsighted, I wasn't that great at cleaning. I went to see the general manager, Bill McReynolds, so that he could hear my interviews. He said I was a good interviewer, but he didn't have a job for me at the station at that time. That left the CBS and ABC local stations. I kept going back, and after a while I knew that CBS was not the right match for me. My destiny was back in the hands of the "not yet" guy Burton LaDow, general manager at the ABC station, KTVK-Channel 3.

That year, 1973, there was a gasoline shortage, and the only way that I could justify looking for a job was to drive to the closest television station to my home, which was ABC. That's where Lynn Castleberry was a big help. She had helped me create the skin-care booklet, and now, as the leader of the 4-H club in Phoenix, she was going to help me start my TV career — only she didn't know it yet. Channel 3 would give a half-hour show to any philanthropic organization that wanted to use the airtime. After I found that out, I went to her and suggested, "Let's do a 4-H half-hour show."

I have a lot of allergies— hay is one of them, as well as grasses and flowers. Let me put it this way: I'm really allergic to a lot of growing things. Needless to say, I was not a good fit for 4-H, but I was going to make this work for me. I researched 4-H up one side and down the other.

We got the time slot from Channel 3, we got kids who were 4-H members, and we put the show together. The kids would submit the projects they were working on, and I would be the judge. One of the projects for the four little 4-H members was cooking. They put the food out, but we misjudged what would happen under the television lights and the food started to congeal. As the judge, I figured I had to taste the food. I was talking to this little girl and she asked, "Are you going to taste my food?" It was macaroni and cheese. I tasted it, and it instantly stuck to the roof of my mouth and made it really difficult to talk.

I turned to the camera and mumbled: "We will be back after these messages." The crew was exploding with laughter because it was really funny. I got the stuff out of my mouth and quickly realized I had to be very careful how I did the rest of the interviews. But I got through it, and now I knew how to deal with congealed food! When we came back from the commercial break, I put the food under my tongue so it didn't stick to the roof of my mouth and I could still talk.

After the show I went to see Mr. LaDow and asked him what he thought. He said he hadn't seen it. As I drove home, I was crushed because I knew the show was good. It was fun, it was light, we got the message out, and we dealt with the ups and downs of the production. I handled everything that happened in that show with ease. I was devastated to find out that the man who might hire me didn't even watch it — that show was my audition tape. I was home for about an hour and the phone rang.

It was LaDow's secretary, who said that he would like to talk to me. "You're not bad. I saw it, I had it taped." I was so naïve that I didn't realize that a general manager of a television station could order a tape of the show from the control room.

Then he said, "You are not bad, but not yet." There again was that "yet." I held onto it, but I was getting discouraged because I knew I could host my own show, or at least thought I knew I could.

One day shortly afterwards, I was talking to my mother, who lived in Denver. I called her a lot to see how she was. I told her about the half-hour show I did and said, "You know, the station is owned by the former governor of Arizona, Ernest McFarland, and is run by this man who I have been meeting with for a year. He keeps saying 'not yet' but I can't get any further."

When my mother repeated the conversation to her best friend Sarah, she said that she knew the governor, and that they were old friends. She then called the governor and said, "You should take a look at this woman, she's really good."

The governor arranged for us to meet. Burton LaDow joined us and acted as if we were meeting for the first time, even though I had met with him once a week for a year about getting my own show. I sat next to the governor, who was about eighty at the time; I was nearly thirty-eight. We talked and he patted my knee. I didn't say anything, and he looked up and said, "Burton, give this girl a show."

LaDow says to me with a straight face, "What kind of show would you like to do?"

I said, "Here, Mr. LaDow, is my format." Finally, at the age of thirty-seven, I had gotten a television show!

The show was called REBA and was on at 2:30 on Wednesday afternoons in the half-hour slot we had used for the 4-H club. LaDow hired me for four weeks. The reason was not that the governor recommended me, but that the National Organization for Women was going to picket the station because it didn't have any women on the air. I had a television show for four weeks at twenty-five dollars a show. Finally, I was doing what I wanted to do.

I was always aware of who was coming to Phoenix for a lecture or a gallery showing. About a month before I went on the air, I went to Burton LaDow and said, "This very famous lady is coming to town. I really would like to interview her while she's here and then run it as one of the shows." He said okay, so a week before I really went on the air (we already had the set) I interviewed Françoise Gilot. I had bought her book to read about her life. My first question: "You have lived with two of the most famous men of the twentieth century. You were Pablo Picasso's mistress and had two children with him, and now you are Dr. Jonas Salk's wife. Being French, does that make you great in the kitchen?"

I knew the answer, because I'd read the book and knew that cooking wasn't her skill. She burst out laughing and said to me, "It wasn't cooking—there were other places where I really excelled." I was watching Burton out of the corner of my eye and he was having a really good time.

So I did my first interview. I knew it was good, and it taught me a lesson. I knew all the answers to the questions I asked because I had read the book. I am a frustrated librarian. I have always enjoyed doing research and it came in handy later in my career. After I got through with the taping, Mr. LaDow came to me and said he thought I should stay for eight weeks. Needless to say, I stayed a lot longer (nearly three years) and I learned a lot on their nickel, or, in this case, their twenty-five dollars.

I kept getting raises because people were actually watching the show, which gave us good ratings. It didn't hurt that both major papers, the *Arizona Republic* and the *Scottsdale Press*, wrote articles about me, my show, and my "Here's Egg On Your Face" speeches for local organizations. I was doing what I loved—giving speeches and hosting a television show.

On the fourth show I got to interview veteran newsman Hugh Downs, who had moved to Carefree, Arizona, a

Phoenix suburb. He was still working in New York but his wife had opened a knitting store, so he would come out to Carefree on weekends. One time when he was there on vacation, he came to the studio on a Wednesday afternoon for a live show. I had researched all of his books and had my clipboard with a list of incredible questions, but during the interview I realized I was more concerned about my questions and was not listening to his answers. I went to a commercial, and when we came back from the break I put the clipboard down and said, "Mr. Downs, you have earned a living in radio and television interviewing. Will you teach me?"

We spent the last half of the show with him giving me advice and me listening. Because I had no clipboard to depend on, I just had a conversation with a very famous interviewer. I absorbed as much as I could. Months later, when I interviewed his wife, Ruth Downs, Hugh joined her. After the interview he said, "Do you know how many people ask for advice?"

I said, "Well, I guess a lot."

"Do you know how many people follow the advice?"

"I have no idea."

He said, "Very few, and you were one of the few. You are turning into a very good interviewer."

By now, I had worked my salary up to fifty dollars a show and within another three months I was up to seventy-five. After a year, I was making one hundred dollars a week at the TV station, I was giving speeches, and I was really, really happy. I was also learning, polishing, and finding out how far I could push myself, as well as how far I could push my guests. Another memorable guest on the show was Robert Ludlum. Knowing that he was an actor before he turned into a very successful writer, I had him read from his book *The Rhinemann Exchange*. Later, Ludlum wrote the Bourne trilogy, so today he's even better known thanks to Matt Damon, who starred in those box-office hits. Luckily for me, he read it as an actor. It was one of the highlights of my show.

Chapter Two

I read that Art Buchwald was coming to town to play tennis at John Gardner's Tennis Ranch. I had met the legendary columnist and humorist many years earlier. Just before we moved to London, we lived in Washington DC, where my husband went to graduate school. One of our friends, Bob Baker, was on loan from the U.S. Information Agency (USIA) to Public Broadcasting for the fundraising auction at the PBS station in Washington, so I offered to help. I had worked as a model and in commercials so I was comfortable on camera. In fact, I had done a great commercial in Washington where I played a suburban sophisticate who was out on the town.

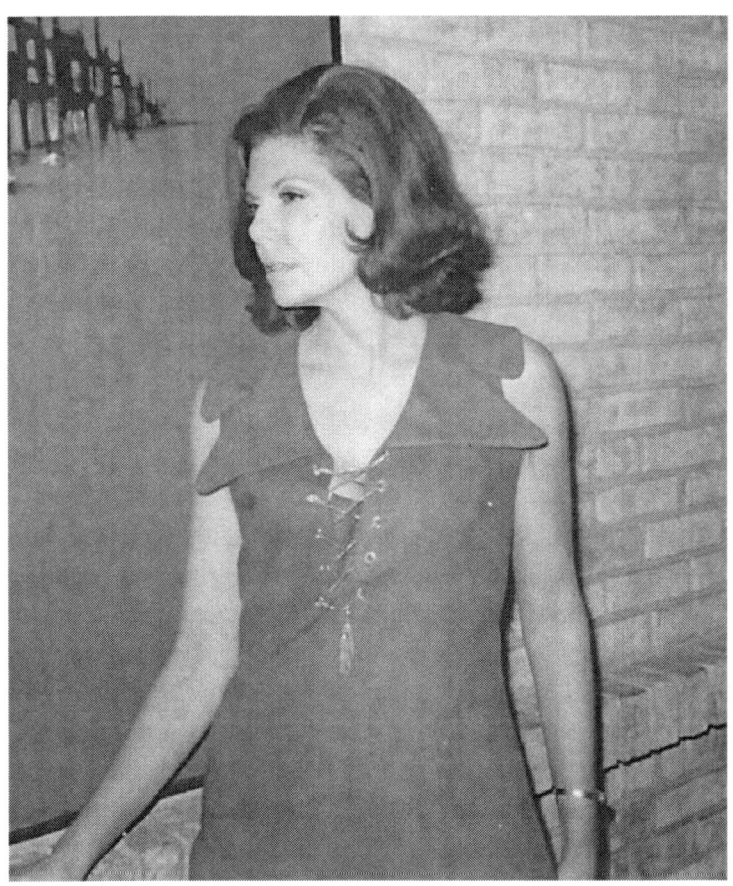

11

Reba Merrill

At the PBS auction, I was the model for Art Buchwald, who was one of the celebrity auctioneers. One of the things I modeled was a brass bra, straight off the cover of Vogue, which I wore over a simple black sheath. The bra attracted a lot of attention, and in the end Art Buchwald bought it. When I read that he was coming to Scottsdale, I sent him a letter and asked if I could interview him. He replied that he didn't think so.

When he got to John Gardner's Tennis Ranch, I called him and said, "I bet you don't remember me, but I was the one who modeled the brass bra. Now I have a television show, could I interview you? I just want to say that we had a lot of fun that week that we worked together on the Public Broadcasting auction." Mission accomplished —he invited me to interview him at the Tennis Ranch. I read all his columns and asked questions about them so he could answer with the punch line. It was really charming and funny. When you interview somebody who's brilliant and bright and humorous, it makes your job a lot easier.

Considering that Phoenix is not Los Angeles or New York, I still got to interview many famous people for my little local show. One interesting guest was Phoenix-native Rusty Warren, frequently called the mother of the sexual revolution. She was known for her songs "Knockers Up" and "Bounce Your Boobies," in which Warren encouraged women to relieve themselves of their bras. She was controversial because her material was considered raunchy for that time, and she talked about sex when the topic was not openly discussed.

Another famous Arizona resident was Amanda Blake, known as Miss Kitty on the TV series *Gunsmoke*, who was generous in telling stories about her costars and the series. She starved for twenty years to fit into the corsets for her costumes. *Gunsmoke* had ended by 1976 and Amanda had moved to Scottsdale, gained twenty pounds and was loving every minute of her freedom.

What a surprise when one of my idols consented to be on my show—Erma Bombeck, a neighbor and one of the funniest and famous writers of that time. I also interviewed Lainie Kazan when she appeared at the Playboy Club in her own performance area, "Lainie's Room."

Not all of my interviews were from the world of show business. One of my guests talked about marriage and sex with great authority, Dr Joyce Brothers. Her advice had been a big help in keeping my marriage afloat for many years. When it came to famous neighbors, one of the most exciting was Buster Crabbe, whom I met at a charity event in 1976. I invited him to be on the show; he was reluctant, but I kept asking, and finally he accepted. He had so much fun and felt so comfortable with me that he invited me to go to Tulsa, Oklahoma to co-host a TV series with him about old Westerns. He had starred in some very low-budget "Billy the Kid" films and knew about Western stars, and he actually knew William Boyd (the actor who played Hopalong Cassidy) and Tom Mix. It turned out that Buster Crabbe was the only actor to play Tarzan, Buck Rogers and Flash Gordon, three of the top pulp-fiction heroes of the 1930s.

I was meeting interesting people, doing incredible interviews, and just having a good time. I was very comfortable and building my brand, and people knew who I was. I was invited to the Playboy Club when it opened and to all kinds of events and parties. I was invited to John Gardner's Tennis Ranch, though I didn't even know how to play tennis, and I met the president of CBS at a party there. During my second year doing my show REBA, I was named to the Governor's Commission on the Status of Women, along with Sandra Day O'Connor, who went on to be the first woman on the Supreme Court. I had had thyroid cancer in 1968, and wherever we lived in the United States, I always volunteered for the American Cancer Society. Lots of people knew who I was: I was Reba Merrill and I was on the ABC station.

All of a sudden things got to feel very strange at the station, and I didn't know what was going on. I had worked there for nearly two years and didn't know if I was getting fired. One day I interviewed a very famous psychic who was in town. His name was Peter Hurkos, and his forte was psychometry, the ability to see past, present and future by association with an object he touched that meant something to you. I had a ring that I have had for a long time and always wore it when I did the television show. He said he'd do the reading for me off-camera.

We did the psychic reading after the show was over and everybody had left the studio. I took off the ring and handed it to him, and he said, "You're going to have an amazing career, but this part of your career is going to change." Of course, I thought that he meant I was going get fired. It felt like another "yet" in my life. I didn't tell anybody what he told me.

Shortly after this, I was called in to Mr. LaDow's office, and he said to me, "We have decided to do a morning show called *Good Morning Arizona*, to follow *Good Morning America*, and you're going to co-host it and produce it." By then, as I mentioned, I was earning one hundred dollars a week, and visions of a big raise went through my head. I thought I would get $500 to do this.

But then he said, "And by the way, we are going to pay you $125 a week." This got me back to twenty-five dollars a show. My (male) co-host was married with children, just as I was, only he got three times the salary. All he had to do was show up to do an interview, that was all. I put the show together, I did most of the interviews, and he got all the money. The reason I was given was that I was married and my husband took care of me, and he had to take care of his family. I loved what I was doing so I didn't care. I never made a career decision based on money.

The reason having my own money was so important to me was because when I was a single mother, it was difficult to rely only on a checkbook with two little girls, Diana, six, and Cheryl, four, to support. One of the stories my younger daughter Cheryl likes to tell is how "creative" we had to become to make our budget stretch. When we were living in Denver, I discovered a Mexican restaurant with an "all you can eat" buffet, and children ate free. One of the items offered was Saran-wrapped burritos that we stuffed into my large fake-leather tote bag. We kept going through the line and getting as many burritos as we could fit in the bag, and that's what we ate when times got tough. Now we can look at this memory as one that brought us together, just like driving in our old car when we would sing the song from the musical *Gypsy*, "Wherever we go, whatever we do, we're gonna go through it together."

Now, in Phoenix, I was finding a voice and a career, and I wanted to see what I could do to give back. I discovered that there was a halfway house, the North Mountain Behavioral Institute, for recovering female drug addicts, and I volunteered to teach them how to do makeup and how to dress, so that when they went back into the real world they would have a sense of well being. I would go to all the department stores and get them to supply me with all kinds of makeup that they were going to throw out. After six months they asked me to be on their board.

Back to finances again. When I had gotten divorced in Denver, all of my credit cards were taken away since I was a single mother with no income and was considered a credit-card liability. Also on this board was a banker from the largest bank in Arizona, and I said to him, "I would like a credit card."

He replied, "The next time we meet, I will bring all the papers," and he did. Then he told me that my husband had to co-sign them.

I responded, "No, you don't understand. I want a credit card in my own name. And if you don't do this, I will do a segment on my show and let them know all about your bank and what you don't do for women." Well, needless to say, I got a credit card, with a limit of $250.

He gave me a piece of advice: "Go out and spend as much of that $250 as you can, then pay it off every month." I did exactly as I was told, then promised myself that no man would ever take credit cards away from me again because I would always have my own credit.

Looking back, I see that the drive I had to succeed came from those moments. I knew I wanted to protect and take care of my children, but what I didn't know was how long it would take me to be successful. By the time I did finally succeed, the drive itself had taken over, and I would put those I loved on the back burner because my career had become the most important thing in my life.

Each of these little steps showed me what I was capable of doing, who I was capable of being, and why I was in Phoenix, Arizona, much to my chagrin. One day I interviewed a guest who had just come from San Diego. After the interview he said, "You know, you're really a lot of fun, and the CBS station in San Diego is looking for someone for the morning show. They're going to replace the co-host and are looking right now."

I sent them a montage of my interviews. The best way to describe my rejection was to say that the tape came back so fast that the ink wasn't even dry on the package I sent. I didn't think too much about it until I got a phone call and they asked me to send another tape. I sent a second tape with my Art Buchwald interview. I didn't hear a word from them, and I didn't know at that point that I was going to need another job soon. *Good Morning Arizona* lasted for six months, and then the station decided to run cartoons in our time slot. Cartoons cost much less money than live TV shows.

Chapter Three

The summer after I got fired from KTVK in Phoenix, my husband had a Dartmouth reunion that I really didn't want to attend, so we made a deal: he would treat me to a week in New York if I would go to the reunion in New Hampshire with him. After the reunion, I went to New York and, because I had worked for ABC, I decided I wanted to meet with Bob Shanks, the creator of *Good Morning America*, probably one of the greatest programmers at the time.

One advantage of being a big shot at the ABC network was that your office was on a very high floor. I got on an elevator to the fifty-sixth floor. The only other person on the elevator asked me where I was going. I said, "I'm on my way to meet with Bob Shanks. I used to work for ABC in Phoenix and I want to see what kind of options are open to me."

Dumb me. I went in, had the meeting, and got him to autograph his book but left there without another job. I was so naïve that I had thought that since I came from a local ABC station, doors would open for me to work at the network.

When I was leaving the building, I ran into the man from the elevator again, and he invited me to lunch. Over lunch he asked, "What are you going to do now?"

I said, "I don't know. I have a week in New York that my husband treated me to."

He said, "Well, it just so happens that HBO is looking for an interviewer to do a presentation on cable, which is to be given to the Lionel Van Deerlin Congressional Committee on Cable Regulations."

So this man, whose name I can't even remember, took me to meet with Russell Karp, president of TelePrompTer Corporation; Gerald Levin, president of HBO who eventually became the chairman of Time Warner; and Steve Elliot from Screen Gems. These were the men who were going to decide who would conduct the interviews. They talked to me and gave me the job. I didn't have to do anything for the production except the actual interviews, and they set those up for me. I interviewed cable subscribers, actors, and producers, and even the flamboyant film director Otto Preminger. They put me up at a hotel, paid all my expenses, and actually paid me for the six weeks I spent in New York City doing the interviews.

The highlight of all of this was that it took place in 1976, the United States Bicentennial. There were a lot of parties in New York to celebrate the Fourth of July.. I was working with a man from an advertising agency who was also involved with the HBO cable project, and he invited me to go to a party at the World Trade Center to see the Tall Ships in a parade. Then he said, "You know, there is a private party here tonight. Would you like to come back and see the fireworks?"

I answered, "Yes, that would be lovely."

All the traffic was tied up in New York; we had to get from the hotel to the World Trade Center and back on the subway. This was probably one of the most exciting nights of my life. I met some of the most famous people in the world. There were more politicians from the White House and Congress than movie stars. Secretary of State Henry Kissinger was there, and so was political historian Arthur Schlesinger Jr. We could see the Statue of Liberty and all the fireworks and ships out on the water. It was the only time in my life that I ever got to look down on the fireworks. It was really an amazing night.

At the time, I didn't realize how important cable television was going to be. HBO, which is now one of the largest and most prestigious cable networks, offered me a job doing interstitial pieces, which are interviews to be played between movies. Coincidentally, that is where my celebrity interviews would air a decade later. In 1976, cable television was just getting started, and I wasn't impressed that HBO had offered me a job. At that time, HBO was just playing a lot of movies; they didn't have any original programming. I didn't take the job because it would have been impossible for me to work in New York and commute back to where my family lived in Paradise Valley, Arizona.

Nearly Famous

When I returned from the high of my trip to New York, I was so depressed that I just sat on the floor all day. A very good friend of mine, an artist named Agnesa Udinotti, offered, "I'm going to California, I have things I want to do [more romantic than business-related], and I'll drop you off in L.A."

I said, "I don't know anybody in L.A."

She remembered that there was a woman who had been a guest on my show who had invited me to come out to L.A. and visit her. There was also an agent in L.A. who kept calling me. He had heard about me and he kept calling me, but I never went to California and had no idea that he was very famous. I decided to go to L.A. The lady, the guest on my show, let me stay at her house in the flats of Beverly Hills. I laugh at myself looking back, now that I live in L.A.; I know exactly where I stayed, but at the time I had no idea where I was.

I set up an appointment with Noel Rubaloff, who was the agent. I arrived at his office, which was very, very large and had a huge desk. Across the room were a leather couch and an end table with a phone. He asked, "Well, what have you been doing?"

I said, "Nothing, but I want to get another television show."

"How can you get another TV show if you have not done anything about it?"

"Well, I still have one tape out at KFMB, in San Diego."

He wrote me a script and gave me the telephone number, and I made the phone call and said exactly what was written on that script. I called Jules Moreland, the program director at the CBS station in San Diego at that time: "I'm going to be in San Diego in a couple of days. Do you think I could stop by and say hello?"

When he said yes, I suggested, "Is there any chance we could have lunch?"

He said, "Absolutely not."

I replied, "That's okay, I'll be there."

I flew down to San Diego only to see him. I got there about 11 o'clock. I was really lucky; the station was not that far from the airport. I went in and met with him. We started talking, and the time just flew by.

He said, "Come on, let's go grab a bite." So we had lunch, and afterwards, as we were walking back, he said to me, "I want you to come into the studio and I want you to interview me." With no time to prepare or do any research, all I knew was that he was the Program Director.

I decided to base my interview on the responsibility of television when it comes to violence. It was a very long interview, and at the end all he said was, "Thank you very much. By the way, you're in the finals. We are making a decision and will call you on Monday."

I flew back to L.A. and then home. When Monday came, I sat by the phone all day. They didn't call.

The conversation around the dinner table was all about HBO. I really wanted my marriage to survive, and I didn't think working in New York would allow that to happen. We talked about it so much that you would have thought I had taken the job.

On Tuesday, after the CBS station failed to call, I went out and ran all the errands that I didn't get to do on Monday. I was out when they did call and our eleven-year-old son Mark answered the phone. They said that it was KFMB calling from San Diego about the possibility of a television show. My son replied, "I don't think she's interested, she's had an offer from New York."

Out of the mouths of babes! I could not have said that myself. When I finally got back and he gave me the message, I called back and they said, "We'd like you to come out tomorrow."

I said, "I'm terribly sorry, I can't be there until Thursday."

Their response: "Fine."

The reason I didn't want to go out the next day was that I wanted to get my hair done, make sure I had the right dress, practice my makeup, and make the best impression possible.

I arrived at the San Diego TV station on Thursday

afternoon. They asked if I would interview one of their reporters, who was covering a murder investigation.

While researching the story, he had gone through the trashcan of the woman who was going to be indicted for murder. He found incriminating evidence and read it live on air, then turned it over to the district attorney. I based my interview on whether she could have a fair trial with all this publicity. I was watching the signals for how much time I had left, and towards the end, I switched the conversation to a more personal note. He was Hispanic, so I asked him, "Please tell me, what's machismo?"

He smiled and said, "The best way to describe it is that we like our women in the kitchen and the bedroom, and not in the boardroom."

I replied, "Thank you, and we'll be right back."

I surprised everyone that I was able to switch topics. I was cool and comfortable. Little did I know that the interview was being viewed by as many women as they could find, many of whom were the wives of the executives at the television station as well as other women who worked there. That afternoon they offered me a position on Sunup San Diego. I had been approved by the co-host, Mel Knoepp, who acted as if he liked me because when we sat on the couch together I appeared much shorter. I have very long legs and a short body, so when we had to stand up together, I had to take off my shoes.

That was the beginning of my hour television show, five days a week at the CBS station in San Diego. When they offered me the job, they asked me two questions: what was I was earning and what was my age? I was so embarrassed about the amount I was earning in Phoenix ($125 a week) that I tripled it, but I told the truth about my age, which was the first big mistake I ever made in my career. On television it didn't matter how good I was or that the viewers loved me—all they could see was my age. Even though I was forty-one, I beat out everyone else, especially the young women just out of college.

I finally had the challenge of doing an hour TV show, five days a week, which was brand new for me. It was an interesting, exciting, and scary time, but deep down I really loved it.

Reba Merrill

It never dawned on me that my co-host wouldn't like me. I didn't understand why, but I guess at times I can be quite intimidating even though I don't mean to be. I thought we got along very well. What surprised me the most was when I got a phone call one day from a woman who said to me, "Who do you think you are? I have sent you so many invitations to come to my organization and speak, and you have never responded."

That was when I found out that my co-host was not telling me about all the invitations, and everybody in San Diego thought that I was a snob or too important or busy for any of the organizations. I knew that in local television you had to make yourself available to anybody who wanted you to speak at their luncheons, dinners or teas—whatever they asked you to do. You did it, and you did it lovingly, which I did when I finally got the invitations.

At the end of one of the shows, I said, "My son ran a race and he received the Slow Turtle award because he was the last one to finish. I am so excited because my son is an asthmatic." I think I was off the air no more than five minutes when I got a phone call from the National Jewish Hospital in Denver. They have a branch in San Diego, and they are one of the biggest hospitals that treat asthma. They asked me if I would come and speak at their luncheon. I was very excited to do this because my sister was a severe asthmatic and owed her life to their hospital. That's the funny thing about life—things pop up when you least expect them.

Nearly Famous

Chapter Four

Working at KFMB was great. I loved it. I interviewed a lot of really famous people. How was I supposed to know when I sat down with Peter Finch, star of the film *Network*, that he would die three weeks after I did the interview? He was given a posthumous Oscar for playing Howard Beale, the character remembered for his "I am mad as hell" speech. He sent me a thank you note, but unfortunately I didn't keep it.

I interviewed Anne Baxter from *All About Eve*, who had written a book about her life. It was so early in TV publicity for the movies that they used to send the big movie stars to us at Channel 8 to let them practice before they appeared on the network shows in New York. Being a fan of movie stars, I was having the time of my life. My co-host didn't want to do interviews like that because they were soft and silly but for me, they were a dream come true.

When I went to Los Angeles to do the interviews for *The World's Greatest Lover*, starring Gene Wilder and Dom DeLuise, I interviewed Dom first. In the interview, he talked about loving to go to the beach. Because he was very fat, I asked, "Do you wear a bathing suit?"

"Of course," he replied, "Don't you know fat people do take off their clothes in public?" Before I could say anything, he started to strip, ending up nude behind the couch we were sitting on and singing to me.

When I went to interview Gene, he stood up and said, "Come in, I have been expecting you," and he started to unzip his pants. "I have heard that the only way to do an interview with you is naked."

Once the laughter had subsided, the ice was broken and I got a really great interview. A short time later, Dom DeLuise went on the *Tonight Show* and told Johnny Carson that he did his first nude interview with some redhead from San Diego. I was ecstatic to be mentioned on national TV, even though I was the only one who knew he was talking about me.

Reba Merrill

I loved my life at that time. During the week, I hosted my TV show in San Diego, and on some weekends I would fly up to Los Angeles and do interviews with stars in films that a studio was promoting. One of the first interviews I did was for a small film called *Star Wars* with an unknown actor by the name of Harrison Ford. I found that segment years later and saw how

badly I did during that interview; I'll tell you more about it later on. I didn't have any time to do research or prepare questions from the information in the press packet. It was a good lesson because it taught me this was not the way I wanted to conduct interviews, and I made sure that in the future I did my homework.

Some of the people I interviewed were Beverly Sills, Lily Tomlin, Susan Sarandon, and the author Sidney Sheldon, who wrote dozens of best sellers and created *Charlie's Angels*.

San Diego was a wonderful place to live. My husband took flying lessons and would fly in from Phoenix most weekends with our son. As far as I was concerned, this was the best of all worlds. Then things started to get strange again at the station. They stopped giving me books to read by authors who were going to be on the show, and nobody would talk to me or to my co-host. I knew what was happening. I said to my co-host Mel

Nearly Famous

Knoepp, "I think this is it. We are going to be fired tomorrow and I am going to say goodbye to our audience."

I said goodbye on the air and he didn't. General manager Robert Meyers personally fired us. The station was very surprised because they got a lot of letters after I was let go. The reason had a lot to do with my age. I was now well over forty-four and was replaced by a twenty-two-year-old. I think that says it all.

Fortunately, I didn't get depressed, as I had the first time I lost a television show. I sent out tapes and got a response from KDKA in Pittsburgh. I went to Pittsburgh and spent a week there. I loved the station, but I was now too much of a West Coast woman to work on the East Coast. I decided to try to convince the local San Diego Cox Broadcasting cable station to let me do a show. It was public access, which meant that normally, anybody could do a television show if they paid the station. I didn't actually pay them. They hired me and paid me fifty dollars a show. I had to do five shows in one day and barter the set; a furniture store created the set in return for a credit on the show.

I went to San Diego State College, hired five interns, and

said to them, "Each one of you is responsible for a show. We will meet once a week and set up what shows we will do. Then you will put them together and we will get the guests." One of

Reba Merrill

my interns, Lu Murray, went on to become a senior supervising producer on *Entertainment Tonight,* and I am so proud of her.

It was 1979. I was flying by the seat of my pants, but for some reason lots of people wanted to be a guest on the show. The daily newspapers were kind to me, which helped the viewers find the show. The show was called *That's Life*. I loved it. It was everything I had dreamed of doing when I started on television. I met all kinds of people, including the former governor of California, Pat Brown. Not all of them were really famous, but everybody had a story to tell. All had overcome serious obstacles or figured out how to get around them. For once in my life, I got to do the kind of television I've always wanted to do.

I had been doing the show for about seven or eight months when I decided to interview more controversial guests. My friend Reverend McKenna from AME Baptist Church suggested that I interview his mother. She was the granddaughter of a slave and the great-grandmother of children going to UCLA. As far as I was concerned, she was in the catbird seat of life, because she saw both sides of the Black Experience, which was the title of the show that featured her interview. I wanted to do this right,

so I went to an African-American sociologist in San Diego and asked what I should ask her. One of the questions was how she felt when two white men came to her door and threatened to evict her. She had twelve children, yet she had the courage not

Nearly Famous

to leave. Her husband was a shoemaker and an itinerant preacher who traveled most of the time. She took care of the children by herself, making and selling sweet potato pies and quilts. I didn't know the right words to use to ask how she felt about what happened to her. The sociologist said I had to use the n-word, which I normally never used. He said that when I asked the question I should put my hands up as if I were doing quotation marks. I asked him to please come to the taping because I was scared to death to do it; little did I know that this wonderful woman would hold my hand through the whole interview. So when I asked the question, I could only put up one hand, one air quote. It was an amazing moment in my life. She answered my question in a small voice: "I didn't like it." She seemed to visibly shrink before my eyes.

The following month, I decided that I really wanted to push the limits. We found three wealthy women who were drug addicts, hooked on pills and getting prescriptions from several doctors. I thought of drug addicts as hookers and thieves, but these women could have been my next-door neighbors. I opened the show by saying, "I'm not a drug addict. I'm just cheap." Then I opened bottles of expired prescription drugs that I had never thrown out and spilled out a lot of pills.

As I said, this was in 1979, but we were doing stories that could be right out of today's headlines. Then I interviewed female alcoholics. They never had a drink until after they had carpooled their children from school—then they immediately broke out the booze. When their husbands came home, they would say, "I was just mixing a drink, would you like one?"

The next guests were lesbians. I knew nothing about being lesbian, but I thought it would make an interesting show.

I had finished the five shows for the week when the general manager pulled me aside and said, "God does not want these tramps on the air."

I replied, "I didn't know I had to answer to God. I thought it was only the FCC." Then he fired me.

I was really surprised when this job didn't work out. I went on to win an Emmy for the Black Experience show months after being fired. I won as the producer and got my own Emmy statue. The irony of all this was that the man who fired me ordered another Emmy statue to display in his office! And frankly, I didn't think that was fair since he didn't like my show.

The San Diego Emmy nominations were judged in Chicago that year. A panel of TV professionals voted on the quality of the show and didn't care if it was from a cable station. So I won an Emmy. The show I was previously fired from at Channel 8 was also nominated for Emmys that year, but they didn't win anything.

Chapter Five

I didn't know what to do next. It was now late summer in 1980, and I wanted to work but couldn't find a job. I started doing PR for a while in San Diego while applying for jobs all over the country. I received seventeen rejections.

It took fifteen months after I was fired from my last job to get the courage to look for work in L.A. Los Angeles was unlike anything I had ever experienced, so I would just travel back and forth from San Diego to L.A. because I was scared to death of being rejected there too. The wonderful agent Noel Rubaloff, who was so instrumental in getting me the talk show in San Diego, had passed away. I didn't know anybody else in L.A. All I knew was that I could interview famous people and get them to say small, intimate things about their lives and careers on camera, and that's what I wanted to do. I was fascinated with how people coped, especially when they were hit with drastic changes in their lives, but when I was confronted with my own obstacles, I didn't know how to deal with them.

I knew I wanted to work in television, but I was already considered too old to be on camera since I was now a woman of a "certain age." Coming to terms about not working on camera ever again was one of the hardest experiences of my life. I liked being a TV personality, particularly in San Diego. I spent a week looking in a mirror and asking myself if I could give up the perks of being an on-camera personality. It wasn't just the invitations to every opening, whether it was the Old Globe Theatre, the opera, or other cultural events. I loved being somebody. At that time, there was no way to be over forty and still work on TV, unless you were really famous at the national level like Barbara Walters. My life as I knew it was going to change forever, and change scared me.

When my husband treated me to a week in L.A., I realized that this was where I needed to go to network with people who could give me a job. Milton Rich, a press agent who worked for CBS in New York and used to bring people out to my television

Reba Merrill

show in San Diego, told me, "I know somebody in L.A., Barbara Claman. She's a very well known casting director, and I will ask if you can stay with her."

He did what he promised, and in return for staying at her house, all I had to do was pick up her groceries and her dry cleaning. I slept on the sofa bed in the den. I didn't have to do anything else, and it gave me time to figure out how to get a meeting at a studio for a job interviewing behind the camera. In the past, when I called up any studio and said, " I am Reba Merrill from CBS (or Cox)," somebody always took my call. Now nobody was taking my calls.

I've never made a work decision based on salary. Money was never something that drove, enticed, or even excited me. What did excite me was being challenged. I realized that by working on a press junket, which the studios arranged to promote their upcoming films, I could get a one-on-one interview with a movie star and not have to be on camera, which was the answer to growing older on TV. When I worked for CBS, I discovered that the secret to a good interview was to get the stars in the middle of the junket before they got tired, and while they were still excited to be there. Only fifty TV journalists were invited to the press junkets, even though, at the time, there were sixteen hundred TV stations across the country.

My colleague from CBS put me in a room at 20th Century Fox with a telephone and a book that listed every television station in the United States. I started calling. I contacted two hundred stations in a week and asked the same question: "Would you take canned material from Hollywood?"

If they said yes, I pounced, "I will be your Hollywood producer—just tell me what you want." Whether I called New York, Philadelphia, or even Des Moines, Iowa, they all wanted the same thing.

They would say: "Give us the movie star. We will take the hype if you humanize it." I knew what the product was, I knew how to make it, and now all I had to do was figure out was how to get somebody to pay for it.

Nearly Famous

As a result of my networking, best-selling author Irving Wallace's publisher called me and asked me to interview Wallace about his latest novel and distribute it to the TV stations. I hoped the stations would play it, and they did, which surprised me because I thought they were only interested in movie stars. Doubleday paid me $5,000, so now I knew producing celebrity profiles could work.

I must have been really naïve. I had already hosted four talk shows, won an Emmy, and done countless interviews, but I wasn't prepared for a meeting I had at 20th Century Fox in late 1982 with a very powerful and rotund man. He looked at my tape and told me I was a very good interviewer. In fact, he said, "You look like you came from central casting. You are what an on-camera interviewer should look like."

I thought this was really interesting because of the seventeen rejections I'd recently received. I didn't say anything, and he continued: "Let's have dinner and discuss what you can do for me because I can give you all the work you can handle."

I was excited: this might be my big break. We had dinner, and when dessert was served, he said, with a straight face, "I will give you all the interviews you want to do, and all you have to do is go down on me three times a week." I thought it was a joke, but he was serious. I just laughed and stalled.

For a week I thought about what to do and decided he was so fat and disgusting that he probably needed me to stroke more than his ego. No job was worth it. Being honest with myself, I thought, if he were better looking I might have been willing to consider it. I wanted to work again, and the fear of never being hired had started to consume me. Was this what it was going to take to work in Hollywood? And why pick me? I was forty-seven and there were lots of younger and prettier women in town. I decided I wasn't going to go the "casting couch" route to get a job, which clearly was not dead in Hollywood. At my second meeting with him, I found the courage to say no, even though I didn't know at the time how I would find another way into the studios. I never worked with him, but I kept my integrity, marriage and my self-esteem intact. I didn't work at

20th Century Fox until eight years later when Teri Ritzer became vice president of international publicity in 1990 and hired me.

It never dawned on me that somebody would look at me at forty-seven and attach sex to giving me a job. After that experience, I started eating candy—not a lot at first—and put on a little weight, eventually becoming addicted to sugar. I told myself and my family, "Now no one will hit on me for work." I was surprised about how I handled that experience. I thought I was stronger than that.

That life-changing experience of being propositioned to get a job was just the beginning of not knowing how Hollywood worked and the games that were played. I had faith in myself and I knew that I could do a good job. I found out that the people sitting behind the desk sometimes used their power in very nasty ways. Later, sex was not the problem—power plays were. It was the women, for the most part, who played the big games, the worst games, and the meanest games.

Chapter Six

Since I couldn't get anybody at a studio to take my calls, I joined a networking group called the Woman's Underground. Everybody there was employed, but looking to move up the corporate ladder. In 1983, not a lot of women had powerful jobs in Hollywood. Most were assistants or had entry-level jobs in the entertainment industry. This group never betrayed the secrets we discussed regarding how or where we were looking for work. Finally, at one meeting, I stood up and said what I wanted: "I am good at what I do and I can't get anybody to give me a chance."

A woman in the back who I will never forget, Beverly Walker, called out: "You have to know somebody who deals with a studio in the division that you want to work for."

I only knew one person who worked in marketing and publicity, Chris Arnold. He used to run the TV crews when I was doing the press junkets, and now he was a big success making movie trailers for the studios. The trailers came out of the marketing division, which is where I knew that video publicity was going to come from too. I wanted to do movie star interviews with clips from the film, plus photos and behind-the-scenes footage. I already had television stations lined up that were willing to take my video celebrity profiles; I just needed to know how to get paid. I called Chris and we had lunch. I said, "I would like to partner with you on video publicity. I know this is going to work. When you get a job to produce a film trailer, try to get them to hire you to do the video publicity too."

Three weeks later he got us our first job. The film was *Cujo*. The movie, based on a novel by Stephen King, was about a rabid dog that kills people. I got to interview Dee Wallace, one of the stars. She told me, "At first, I turned *Cujo* down because I didn't think I was strong enough to tackle it. It would take everything I had emotionally and physically. They treated me for exhaustion for two months afterwards…But when I think of the best mile I could run, I think of *Cujo*."

Because there was no behind-the-scenes footage from the set of the film, I would just do a video profile and attach it to clips from the movie. Dee graciously agreed to let us do the interview at her home and shoot some behind-the-scenes footage there. We videotaped her walking with her husband by the pool and showed her scrapbook of other film and TV roles, and then we shot the walls in her home where she had the poster from the film *E.T. the Extra Terrestrial*. She had played the mother in that film. She also had the poster from *10*, starring Bo Derek, in which she had a small role.

That was all the footage I could get, but I was still able to produce a celebrity profile that the TV stations would air. My interview with Dee gave me my start doing celebrity profiles and the chance to prove that television stations would take canned material from Hollywood. The interview got played on two national TV shows, *Entertainment Tonight* and *Night Flight*, and was the catalyst for everything that happened in my career for the next two decades.

We came back to the office and I did a paper edit, which is an outline that is used by the videotape editor. Chris Arnold's company, Cimarron, finished editing the video profile. The stations not only played it, but they also sent back cards telling us how they played it. The first celebrity profile I ever did was five minutes and a few seconds long, cut into two-and-a-half-minute segments and run for two nights. The stations ran video publicity on the noon and evening news, or on their a.m. or p.m. talk shows, whichever show they had on the local station; in other words, they always found a way to use it. They would replace my voice on the tape with their own reporter's. I know of one TV reporter who went to the trouble of shooting some video of herself that she used in the profile to look as if she had done the interview, and was fired for lying about it. We sent it to the fifty-five television stations I had contacted. The stations sent me copies of the segment, called air checks. They don't send them out anymore, but in 1983 I got air checks so I could see how the stations were using our segments.

After the local stations started playing my video profile on *Cujo*, my son said to me, "You're nothing, Mom, if you're not on *Night Flight*," which was a weekly variety show on the USA cable network that ran short films, hot musical acts, and videos. I sent them my profile on *Cujo* and got my first national air play.

When I called Stu Samuels at *Night Flight*, he said, "Who the hell are you? I never get anything like this from Hollywood. I will play anything you produce." And he did, until the show ended in 1988. I have my son Mark to thank for the idea of submitting my work to Night Flight and starting a professional relationship with Stu that has lasted over twenty-five years.

After doing the video publicity for *Cujo*, I didn't feel like I was truly a partner with Chris. Warner Bros. Studios paid his company, Cimarron, and I got 10 percent of the amount, so I decided to find someone else who would hire me. I went to the biggest movie trailer maker in town, Andy Kuehn, who had a company called Kaleidoscope. I showed him the celebrity profile for *Cujo* and said to him, "I could run a division for you and do video profiles of the stars that are in the trailers that you are producing."

He answered, "Okay, let's try."

The first movie we worked on was *The Natural* with Robert Redford and Glenn Close. Andy already had a contract to produce a network special and the trailer for The Natural, and he had already shot footage on the set of the film. Since he had one day left of shooting for the special, he asked me to come along to the set and remarked, "Maybe after my interview with Redford, we will have enough time for you to ask him a few questions for a celebrity profile."

I had never been on a film set before, so I didn't know how to dress. I decided that if I was meeting Robert Redford, I'd better dress up. I wore high boots with super-high heels and a silk dress. No one had told me to wear comfortable shoes and washable clothes, because the floors on a set are made of cement and there's a lot of dust and dirt. Sets are being built around the actors, and there are very few places to sit down. The next time I went on a film set, I knew how to dress as well as how to act.

When you work on any film set, the first person you meet is the unit publicist; then they introduce you to the first A.D., the assistant director. You never meet the stars unless the unit publicist first introduces you, even though they know you're coming. There is a protocol you have to follow on a film set. No matter whose film it is, no matter what country you are in, it's always the same.

Glenn Close wasn't shooting that day, so I was interviewing only Redford. By the time I got to sit down to do the interview, there wasn't a part of my body that didn't hurt. I had attended the University of Colorado about the same time that Redford was there on a baseball scholarship. I asked him which bar near campus was his favorite, Tulogies or The Sink, where he worked for a while and was known for his drinking. That made him laugh, and I realized how important it was to break the ice and make the star relax. I did the interview and I loved it.

I interviewed Redford again many years later in 1998 when he directed and starred in *The Horse Whisperer*. I asked how he coped with fame and everyone knowing who he was.

He replied, "So I am not completely overwhelmed by this business, I create another life for myself to go to. I don't much like the business. I like the art of it but not the business…When people recognize you, they are reacting to the person they see on the screen…I try to keep it separate. When I work, I am that guy. When I live my life, I am this guy."

After my first interview with Robert Redford, Andy must have been pleased with me because he said, "Now I want you to interview Paul Newman for *Harry & Son*." Not bad for my first two assignments – Redford, then Newman.

I went out to Malibu where Paul Newman and Joanne Woodward were renting a house. I did my research at the library of the Academy of Motion Picture Arts and Sciences, the people who present the Oscars. In researching the questions for the Paul Newman interview, I discovered that the one movie he hated was his first film role in 1954, The Silver Chalice. I read that he wished he could buy back the print of the film so no one else would ever see it. I found a column by the legendary Hollywood columnist Hedda Hopper saying that when she saw Newman in *The Silver Chalice*, she knew right then that he was going to be a big movie star.

I had the column copied, which cost 25 cents a page at that time. After the interview was over, I asked if he would like to see Hedda Hopper's column. "She loved you after seeing *The Silver Chalice*."

He asked me if he could keep that column, and I gave it to him with pleasure. It was a wonderful experience to meet the handsome leading man, humanitarian, racecar driver, and superstar, who was very open and very charming. Newman, who appeared in over eighty films and TV shows in his acclaimed career, told me, "I like all the preliminary work. I don't know if I like standing in front of a camera. If my work has been done well, it is before we even turn a foot of film."

I also met his wife, Joanne Woodward, who starred with him in *Harry & Son*, which he also directed. She was very gracious and welcomed me into their home, even serving us some refreshments.

"Joanne has an interesting theory," he said. "She thinks one of the reasons I started racing is that I was getting bored with acting, and my passion for racing bled back into my acting... The lady knows me better than I know myself."

I asked him how he handled directing his wife.

"It can be difficult. It can be easy. If it was too easy, it wouldn't be any fun. I know when to keep my mouth shut with her... She blows my socks off."

One of Hollywood's most successful couples onscreen and off, they were married for forty years until he passed away at the age of eighty-three in 2008.

"I think our marriage is successful because we listen a lot. I don't want to give the impression that it is all cherry pie and ice cream. It can be stormy, impossible, difficult, and insensitive, but it is never boring."

The next film I worked on was *Stick*, starring and directed by Burt Reynolds. Andy Kuehn told me that he would go to Florida to interview Reynolds so that he could also visit his mother, who lived there. Andy gave me the interview and footage he shot of Burt at home, as well as behind the scenes footage from the film, called b-roll. The studio gave me the film so that I could pull out some scenes for the profile. After I created a paper edit and the video profile was produced and approved by the studio—everything I worked on had to be approved by the studio—I sent it to the TV stations willing to play the star profile.

I found out later that Andy got paid ten times as much as I did for the three films we worked on together, but at the time I was happy with what I got. When Redford was presented with the special that Andy produced, he didn't approve of it, so the special never aired. Redford only approved my three-minute celebrity profile. Andy then decided that if his special wasn't going to air, then neither was my interview with Redford, so he wouldn't let me send it out to stations. I don't even have a copy of that interview with Redford. That's the power of important people. More lessons dealing with the "power brokers" were yet to come.

Chapter Seven

My drive to succeed in the entertainment industry in Hollywood was so strong that I was willing to do whatever it would take to keep getting hired—except for "genuflecting" to that fat Fox executive, of course. I wanted it so badly I became a people pleaser and would do whatever I was asked. I lied about my age, since I had already been replaced by a younger version of me when I was hosting a talk show. I even lied about the airplay my video profiles were getting; even though the actual 92 percent rate was extraordinary, I told the studios it was 97 percent so that I could look even better!

When you have an addiction, there is a comfort in lying, or at least exaggerating, and I was telling lies about absolutely anything; addicts are very proficient liars. I did have some boundaries. I never took credit for work that wasn't mine or stole work from anyone, but then again, no one was doing the caliber of work I delivered at that time.

I had heard about a woman named Michele Reese who would reach out and help women, which was very rare in Hollywood at that time. I asked everyone I knew if they could introduce me to Michele. At one of the networking sessions, Robert Katz, who many years later would hire me to promote his film *Selena*, introduced me to a man who worked at Avco Embassy. Michele had just left Avco to become a vice president of publicity at Universal Studios.

The man, whose name I unfortunately can't remember even though he was instrumental in my career, said to me, "I hear you want to meet Michele Reese."

I asked if he would introduce me.

He replied, "I'll tell you what I'll do. You take me to lunch and I'll set up a meeting for you with Michele Reese."

He picked The Palm in West Hollywood, which is known for its big steaks, big lobsters, big drinks, and big prices. I had a credit card but I was watching my money very carefully after losing my job in San Diego.

Reba Merrill

My husband thought there wasn't anything I couldn't do, so he challenged me to see if I could make it in Hollywood. As I said earlier, I have always been the kind of woman who likes a challenge, so there was no way that I was going to stop at this point. I met with the man from Avco at the Palm with the hope that he would introduce me to Michele and that there would be no "strings" attached. He had three drinks, and while we were talking, I was mentally adding up the tab at about $8.50 a drink. Remember, this is 1984. Then he ordered a big steak, and I realized that I was in for about an eighty-dollar lunch. I just stuck it out and when the check came, I reached out to take it, and he said, "That's not necessary, I was testing you." He lived up to his word: he got me a meeting with Michele Reese, no strings attached.

When we met in Michele's office, she said to me, "You don't remember me, do you?" I didn't, and it never occurred to me at the time that was why I got the meeting. Could I really have been that naïve? Many years earlier, in the seventies, she had been a guest on my show in San Diego representing the Marine Corps, in a most unflattering uniform and hairdo. Now I was meeting a beautiful, blonde woman wearing a blue angora sweater, black skirt, and high heels.

Much to my surprise, she was willing to hire me and gave me the film *Mass Appeal*, starring Jack Lemmon, for my first celebrity profile on my own. I now had my foot in the door at a major studio and had really "met" the woman who would keep me working on one film after another for years to come.

I showed Michele an air check from a station in Oklahoma of the Dee Wallace interview and a list of fifty-five TV stations that had agreed to play my celebrity profiles. She asked, "How do I know they are going to play everything you send them?"

I said, "Here's the list—call anyone you want." I appeared so confident that I don't think she called anyone.

She told me she would give me a chance, but that she was sticking her neck out for me since no one at Universal knew who I was. She was referring to Edward Roginski, senior vice president of marketing and her immediate boss, who reported to

Marvin Antonowsky, president of marketing. Towards the end of the meeting she said, "If you fail, please have the courtesy not to come back."

I had no intention of failing. As I was leaving she added: "Oh, by the way, don't talk about homosexuality in the Catholic Church," which was the subject of the movie. I was thrilled about this opportunity to work for Universal that paid more money than I'd ever seen in my life.

After getting hired by Michele Reese, I told Andy that I had gotten my first job on my own. He said, "If it doesn't work out, you can always come back."

Working for Andy was a learning experience. He told me, "No matter how long the interview is, look at it as a piece of baloney— only give the studio a three-minute slice." Later I used this advice to generate additional revenue. Steven Panama, who ran the business side of Kaleidoscope, told me that if I didn't put the film through the company, I would not be welcomed back. The lessons kept coming.

In those days, there was no behind-the-scenes footage; everything I used for my profile, I had to create myself. After my meeting with Michele, I was given a telephone number for Jack Lemmon. I called and was told by someone on his staff what day he would do the interview at his office.

I countered, "I don't want to do the interview at the office. I want to do it at his home. My viewers want to see him at home." I forgot that I was interviewing him for a celebrity profile and, at the moment, I didn't have any viewers as I had on my talk show. They asked me to hold the phone, then came back and agreed to let us go to his house in Beverly Hills for the interview.

It was an unbelievable experience. Not only was Jack Lemmon the most charming man, but he gave so much of himself. He laughed and told us stories and played songs he'd composed on the piano so that we wouldn't have to pay clearance fees for music used in his profile. He let me photograph his baby book, caricatures by famed artist Al Hirschfeld, and the photos and posters on his walls, which was really important because there were a lot of pictures from his films, including from *Some Like It Hot*.

Jack was in a blond wig wearing a blue dress; his cohort in crime, Tony Curtis, in a pink dress with red hair. He said it was quite a challenge to dress in drag, and he wasn't sure he could be convincing or that he and Tony Curtis could pull it off.

"Tony got a crazy idea and dragged me into the ladies' room," when they were in costume on the studio lot. "We fussed with our lipstick and fixed our hair as about fifty girls walked in and out, and no one batted an eye. I said, 'We're in.'"

I replied, "You were two of the ugliest girls I'd ever seen on film," at least until *Tootsie* with Dustin Hoffman came out years later.

He told me that he knew he wanted to be an actor from the time he was eight or nine years old. He went to Harvard, taught himself how to play the piano, and in the early 1950s, he appeared in one hundred live TV shows, done in New York at that time. When he got to Hollywood, he made a very positive impression with his first credited role in the film *It Should Happen to You* costarring Judy Holiday in 1954.

Born John Uhler "Jack" Lemmon III, he was asked to change his name before starring in his first film. Lemmon had a contentious meeting with Columbia studio boss Harry Cohn, who feared that critics might make jokes about the name "Lemmon" in headlines panning the film. He wanted Lemmon to change his name to "Lennon." Lemmon countered that if he did that, people might confuse his name with "Lenin" and associate him with communism, a very real concern in the 1950s. He decided to keep the name Jack Lemmon and went on to become a Hollywood legend.

He won his first Oscar as Best Supporting Actor for *Mister Roberts* in 1955, a role that he believed came from a bit of luck. The film's director, John Ford, just happened to see a screen test Lemmon had done playing an eighty-year-old man when he was only in his twenties.

"Ford said, 'I never saw a worse old man, but he would make a great Ensign Pulver.' And I got the part."

He was nominated for a Best Actor Oscar for playing an alcoholic in *The Days of Wine and Roses* with Lee Remick in 1962. He reminisced about the movie *Save the Tiger*, which won him his second Academy Award. His role in the 1973 film touched him and made him aware of his own behavior at home. His character had a drinking problem, which was how he dealt with unhappiness and the fear he was going to lose his company. Jack realized that the character was very close to himself; in fact there were moments when he felt the character had really taken over his life. He told me he still liked to drink, and that when he had too much, he took it out on the walls and doors of his house. He never hit anybody; when his emotions and behavior were out of control, he left holes in his walls.

Although Jack went public with his drinking in the 1960s, it wasn't until three decades later that he admitted on the TV show *Inside the Actors Studio* that he was a recovering alcoholic. I never told anyone up until now what he told me, nor did I show the video with that part of his personal story. It is interesting that his Best Actor Oscar nominations and later winning of the Academy Award were for characters that were alcoholics.

Liza Minnelli and Gregory Peck read the names of his formidable competition at the 46th Annual Academy Awards in 1974 : Marlon Brando for *Last Tango in Paris*, Jack Nicholson for *The Last Detail*, Al Pacino for *Serpico*, and Robert Redford for *The Sting*—and then presented the Oscar to Jack Lemmon for *Save the Tiger*. He said it was one of the most gratifying and emotionally fulfilling performances of his career.

I was very surprised that a two-time Oscar winner would be so gracious and kind, though I should've known, after interviewing Paul Newman, that the biggest stars are often the most gracious, especially to those of us just starting out.

At the conclusion of the interview he said some wonderful things. I said to Jack, "Do you really mean what you're saying to me?" and he said yes.

I asked, "Would you put it in a letter?" And he did. I called his office after I got the letter and asked if I could show it to the studios, and they agreed.

I saw Jack one more time, in 1996 when I was doing video publicity for the film *Getting Away with Murder* that he starred in with Lily Tomlin.

I said, "I don't know if you remember me. I interviewed you for the movie *Mass Appeal* and you sent me this amazing letter. Would you like to read it?"

He answered, "You read it."

I couldn't get through it without crying. I said, "I don't know how to thank you for putting my career on the fast track." I never saw him again. Jack Lemmon passed away from colon cancer at the age of seventy-six in 2001, but his legacy of memorable films and my memory of a generous man live on.

Nearly Famous

JACK LEMMON

August 14, 1984

Dear Reba,

I just wanted to drop you a line and tell you how much I truly enjoyed doing our tape session the other day.

Having been in this crazy business for three decades now, I hate to think of how many interviews of this type I have been involved with in the past, but I can honestly tell you that I have seldom enjoyed one as much as I did ours. First of all, you're bright, you're stimulating, and you really do your home work. Your questions are intelligent and incisive, and I never once felt, "Oh God, here we go with that question again for the 100th time!"

In short, although I don't know how long the session lasted, I could have kept on going with no qualms whatsoever. And believe me, that's not the usual reaction!

Again, my many thanks for making something that is usually work a genuine pleasure.

Please give my very best wishes to your delightful daughter and save some for yourself.

And may the wind at your back never be your own!

Always,

Jack

Ms. Reba Merrill
645 Westmount Drive
Suite 212
Los Angeles, California   90069

Chapter Eight

Interviewing Jack Lemmon was just the beginning of an adventure that would last for twenty-three years. That interview was special: not only was it the first big studio job I'd done on my own, but my daughter Cheryl went with me to the interview. Cheryl would later become the backbone of my business as a self-taught editor who worked on all my celebrity profiles. Once I realized that Cheryl could execute what I wanted without my guidance, I began a trusting her completely.

I stopped doing the paper edits and let her edit the video profiles on her own. I knew that she deserved her own recognition, so when she asked to be hired as my editor, I felt confident that she was the best person for the job, We became a team, not an easy feat for a mother and daughter. My other daughter, Diana, went in another direction and moved to Texas to work for a dress manufacturer. My son, Mark, is an award-winning music editor.

My job was to publicize a movie. The goal was always the same: to get you, the audience, to buy a ticket and see the movie. No matter what the budget of the film, my job was to make you want to see it. I started working for Universal, and they paid me quite a bit of money. When I worked for a major studio, there was more money to put into the production. When I was hired to promote a film from a smaller studio, like New World, I had to make everything look expensive, even though we had much less to spend on the production.

I don't remember how I got my first meeting at New World, a mini-major studio that released mostly low-budget films. I met Bill Shields, who was the president of marketing at New World, at the same time that Michele Reese hired me for *Mass Appeal* at Universal.

It was unusual that I met with the president of a division my first time calling on a studio. Normally, I would have met with the person below him first, but that position had not been filled yet, so Bill was doing double duty. He was running the division and hiring people like me to do video publicity. I don't know what I would have done without people like Bill Shields, who not only hired me when I was just starting out, but also gave me a lot of work.

The first film I worked on at New World was *The Philadelphia Experiment*, which is based on an alleged event in 1943 when the US Navy tried to make the USS Eldridge, a US Navy destroyer escort ship, invisible. The film adds a sci-fi twist to the story, telling the tale of two men from the ship who are sent forty years into the future to 1984. Someone else had shot all the publicity footage and Mr. Shields did not like the way it looked. He brought me in to see if I would do new interviews with Michael Paré and Nancy Allen, the stars of the film. Because the studio did not want to spend a lot of money, we decided to do the interviews at my apartment, rather than rent the hotel room in L.A. that we frequently used, a room set up without any beds.

My first interview was with Michael Paré, who had a reputation for displaying outrageous behavior. Paré arrived with dirty hair, which needed to be washed before he had his makeup done. Fortunately, we had hired a makeup artist who could also do hair. He was so good-looking, yet he seemed totally indifferent about his appearance. Paré was known for his drinking, so we served only food – no alcohol. He had starred in *Eddie and the Cruisers* in 1983, which was a big success and the reason that New World was willing to spend money on his next film, *The Philadelphia Experiment*.

At first, he seemed uncomfortable being interviewed. A lot of really talented actors are often very shy when not playing a character and extremely uncomfortable talking about themselves. I have to say I liked him. He was charming, and once he started talking, he relaxed and it was an enjoyable interview for both of us. His costar, Nancy Allen, arrived for the interview completely made up and beautifully dressed. She was definitely happy to do the interview. Nancy had been married to Brian DePalma and had starred in two of his major films, *Dressed to Kill* with Michael Caine and Blowout with John Travolta.

Nearly Famous

My next film from Universal was *Mask*, starring Cher, and it came just days after working on *The Philadelphia Experiment*. It was a last-minute decision by Universal to submit Cher for

Oscar consideration. That's how Hollywood works: they create a lot of publicity with the hope that their films and stars will be nominated for an Oscar. I was told to do the interview with Cher in the photographer's studio where she was being photographed for the cover of *Us* magazine. There was no behind-the-scenes footage from *Mask*, but we could tape some of the photo shoot. In *Mask*, costarring Sam Elliott and Eric Stoltz, Cher plays a freewheeling biker woman on drugs who fights to get her bright but deformed son the education she feels he deserves.

This was just the beginning of films being marketed with electronic press kits, or EPKs, as they were starting to be called. Instead of the studios having to buy a lot of commercial time to promote their films on a local TV station, they could get free publicity by sending them the video profiles we produced that the audience was more likely to watch than a commercial.

I went to the interview with Cher, not knowing what to expect. I knew her background as a hit recording artist with her then-husband Sonny, and from their TV show in the seventies. Now she was becoming a serious actress. I had seen her in *Silkwood*, costarring with Meryl Streep, and I knew that she was a powerhouse. I thought to myself, "We are just going to have a conversation."

I was surprised that she was so open and would reveal so much about herself. She started off by telling me that she didn't think of herself as a risk taker "because when you've got nothing, you've got nothing to lose. People already didn't think I was talented, so all I could do was confirm their feelings or change their minds." But to me, she was a risk taker.

She was born Cherilyn Sarkisian in 1946, but the world knows her as Cher. When I sat down with her in 1985, she was only thirty-eight but already considered "old" in Hollywood.

I told her, "Whatever you do, don't flaunt your age. It doesn't matter how good you are." I was speaking from experience because I knew how I had gotten judged and eventually fired for my age. The only disappointing thing about this interview was that she had cut off all her gorgeous hair and had short dark hair with a blond streak down the center. I called it the skunk look. I wish she'd had her trademark long hair for the interview, but you don't get everything you wish for.

She told me she grew up in the Central Valley in California and quit school at sixteen to go to Hollywood. She met Sonny Bono in 1963 through mutual friends when she was only sixteen and he was twenty-seven. She had no place to live, so he offered to let her stay at his apartment. It wasn't a proposition, since he thought she was an oddball and he wasn't the least bit interested. At the time, Sonny was working for music producer Phil Spector (who forty-five years later went to jail convicted of murdering his girlfriend). Spector gave Cher some work as a backup singer.

Sonny and Cher became inseparable friends and eventual lovers. They were married after she gave birth to their daughter,

Chastity, in 1969. They invested all their money in their film project, also called *Chastity*, which starred Cher in her first film role, which forced Sonny to pawn a ring to pay for the baby's delivery. Their daughter Chastity made headlines when she legally became Chaz after transgendering into a man at the age of forty-one.

When Sonny and Cher released their first single, "I Got You Babe," in 1965, they hit really, really big. But by the time she was twenty-two in 1968, her music career stalled when their record sales dried up. Cher learned to reinvent herself, which she has done several times throughout her career, and came back three years later with a hit TV show, *The Sonny and Cher Comedy Hour*.

It worked. "Once I got to do *The Sonny and Cher Show*, it was really fabulous to do those sketches. I had a really good time doing them. I did them for a long time, and then I wanted to do something more."

After thirteen years together, Sonny and Cher were divorced in 1975 and she was on her own. As open as Paul Newman and Jack Lemmon were in telling their stories, I just wasn't prepared for Cher being so open and honest. She told me, "The thing that scared me the most was leaving Sonny," and after doing the thing that scared her most, nothing ever frightened her that much again.

After her hit records, sell-out performances in Las Vegas, and a successful TV show, all she wanted now was to be taken seriously as an actress. I got the feeling she never thought of herself as a singer but as an actress, and nobody wanted to give her a break. She got a meeting with theater producer Joe Papp, who said, "How can I take you seriously? Look at all the crap you've done on TV." She didn't let that stop her. She kept pushing and doors started opening.

Director Francis Ford Coppola was scouting locations in Las Vegas and went to see Cher's show. "And afterwards he came backstage and said, 'You are so talented. Why aren't you making movies?' And I said, 'Because nobody thinks I am so talented that I should be making them.' And he responded, 'Well they're wrong. I don't care what anyone says, I'm right and they're wrong.'"

Coppola met with Cher in Hollywood to try to develop some projects, but still nothing came of it. "Then I saw Linda Ronstadt onstage, and I thought, Linda and I come from the same place, I can do this."

And that's when Cher decided that if they wouldn't let her make movies, she would go to New York. She told me she had to give up getting paid $300,000 a week in Vegas and said to herself, "If I really want to do it, it's now or never because I don't have any more time. I didn't have the years you can take when you are twenty. I need to do it now or forget it."

Director Robert Altman gave her the part of Sissy in the Broadway version of *Come Back to the Five and Dime Jimmy Dean, Jimmy Dean* and then cast her in the film version of that play, which earned her a Golden Globe nomination for Best Supporting Actress. Film opportunities finally started coming her way.

Mike Nichols had turned her down in the past, but when he was getting ready to direct Meryl Streep in *Silkwood*, he saw Cher's performance onstage in New York and offered her the role of Dolly in the film, also costarring Kurt Russell. She said she told her sister that she was "scared to death" working with Meryl Streep on only her second major film.

She told me, "I was packing my bags and I said to my sister, 'I'm not going. I can't work with Meryl Streep my second time, I'm just not ready for it. Maybe later, but not now.'"

Her sister said to her, "They saw your work. Let them be the judge."

When Silkwood was about to be released, Cher told me that she and her sister and brother-in-law "ran to the theater" to see the trailer. When her name came up on the screen, the audience laughed.

She told me, "I had to bite the inside of my cheek to keep from crying. I was so upset." Meryl and Cher, who plays a lesbian in the film, were nominated for Oscars, and Cher won a Golden Globe for Best Supporting Actress for that role.

Another thing that surprised me was that she let us film her scrapbook, which showed a lot of the costumes from *The Sonny and Cher Show* and outfits from Las Vegas with millions of feathers. She liked feathers and sparkles.

She also let me photograph her wigs. Why she didn't wear one for my interview I will never know for sure, but I thought it might have had something to do with the look they wanted for the photo shoot for *Us* magazine.

I caught up with her again about ten years later in another film, *Faithful*, costarring Ryan O'Neal, which was a different kind of interview. She wasn't new to the film business anymore and had already won an Oscar for *Moonstruck*, so she had achieved recognition from her peers with the entertainment industry's highest honor. She'd been around the publicity circuit and did not share as much of herself as she did during our first interview.

Cher was miserable while shooting *Faithful*. I don't know why, but she kept avoiding the interview, and it wasn't that she didn't remember me. The studio, New Line, demanded that I copy the film's trailer and just insert sound bites. When I sent the video publicity to the TV stations, they didn't play it since it looked like a commercial. The only sound bite they did play was a quote from Cher about infidelity. She has been linked with many actors and some younger men, but she never married again after divorcing Gregg Allman in 1979. I asked her if she was faithful in relationships, and she said, "If I wanted to sleep with someone else, I just left the one I was sleeping with."

As you will read in this book, I have had the privilege of interviewing the biggest stars in Hollywood, and if you ask me who my favorite interview has been after all these years, I always say Cher. I never had anybody talk to me the way she did, and share so much. You got a glimpse of the real Cher when she gave the eulogy after Sonny died suddenly in a ski accident in 1998. I saw it on TV and it was the most incredible delivery of emotion that I had ever seen. She called Sonny "the most unforgettable character I've ever met."

Reba Merrill

Cher is a good actress, not a bad singer, and underneath the plastic surgery and outrageous costumes, one hell of a lady. Another ten years went by and I went to see Cher perform in her spectacular show at Caesar's Palace in Las Vegas. I sent a note backstage hoping that she would remember me. She didn't, but I will never forget my amazing interviews with a woman who has never given up on herself or her dreams. Perhaps that is why I felt a real connection to her. Despite the many detours and bumps in the road that got me to this point, I never gave up either.

Chapter Nine

My one-hour interview with Cher was so amazing that when the studio saw the profile I produced, they asked if I could create three more instead of just the one. I took Andy Kuehn's advice and cut the interview into three-minute slices, producing four separate pieces for Universal. One video press kit had profiles of Cher and her costars Sam Elliott and Eric Stoltz along with film clips from *Mask*. It was sent to all fifty-five TV stations on my list, and then Universal decided to send it out free on satellite to any station that wanted it. As far as I know, this was one of the first times free film publicity was sent by satellite.

The woman at the Satellite Network sent out postcards to everyone claiming that she had done the Cher interviews. When I found out what she had done, I had my lawyer, Harold Lipton, send her a cease-and-desist letter to stop spreading lies. I thought that would take care of the problem. Instead she decided to get back at me by telling a number of the publicists who handled big movie stars that I was selling my interviews to the TV stations. I didn't find this out until ten years later, when Adam Gordon from Sony International told me what she had done.

As a result of her smear campaign about me with the publicists, I was turned down for some big-star interviews, even when the studio wanted me to do the video profiles. One particular publicist kept refusing my interview requests for Julia Roberts and Sean Connery, though I finally interviewed both of them years later. In true Hollywood fashion, the publicist, whom I will not name but was known for damaging careers, eventually fell from grace. Today she is no longer a power broker. Her client list got much slimmer and she got a lot fatter.

The four video profiles I produced featuring only Cher also were played in heavy rotation on the Z Channel, a defunct cable channel that served the areas around L.A. where the majority of the Oscar voters lived. Despite all the publicity, Cher did not receive an Oscar nomination for *Mask*, although she did win Best Actress at the Cannes Film Festival that year as well as a Golden Globe nomination in 1985.

At the same time that we were working on *Mask*, I was hired by New World to interview Tatum O'Neal for the film *Certain Fury*. I had an interview coming up with Cher's costar Sam Elliott for *Mask*, so we decided to meet with Tatum at the same time. We used just one crew and let Universal pick up the cost because they had more money than New World. Both movies had wrapped, which meant we couldn't go to the set, so we did the interviews at my daughter Cheryl's apartment. It didn't matter where we did the interviews as long as they looked good.

We arranged a beautiful spread of food and had the crew set up for the Sam Elliott interview. He was charming, really a great guy, and exactly what I expected him to be. We waited and waited for Tatum O'Neal. Finally, we called New World and informed them that Tatum never showed up.

New World must have been happy with the job I did on *The Philadelphia Experiment* because they hired me for the dark drama *The Boys Next Door*. This was the first time that I shot all the material used in a celebrity profile. Before working on this film, I had only done the interviews with the stars and shot their personal photos. I was nervous that I might not do it right or get everything we needed to produce the video profile. It didn't help that Charlie Sheen was such a free spirit and that I was so uptight!

I was surprised that I got more jobs from New World after that film. Eventually, I did relax and loosened up after finding the right rhythm for future visits to the sets. I was learning so much about myself. I was willing to fake it until I made it, as they say, and I was willing to fail.

The Boys Next Door starred a very young Charlie Sheen, who was a wild boy on the set, while his costar Maxwell Caulfield was calm, collected, and amused by Charlie's antics. I wonder whether this was a preview of Charlie's later years, when his bizarre behavior would result in his being fired from his hit TV series, *Two and a Half Men*. The film had a dark storyline about two "nice" young men, played by Sheen and Caulfield, who killed gay men. The tag line was: "Young, handsome, desirable, deadly." I want to go on record here and say I didn't MAKE the movies; my job was just to publicize them!

I had no sooner finished *Mask* than Universal hired me again, this time to interview Chevy Chase for *Fletch*. Chevy was so funny that the crew couldn't stop laughing. I had to keep asking the questions over and over again so that we could get some

answers on tape that that weren't ruined by background laughter. This was a challenge because the more the crew laughed, the funnier Chevy tried to be. I was on quite a roller coaster, from the comedic antics of Chevy Chase to the violent *The Boys Next Door*. It was probably New World's most controversial film and quite a contrast to Fletch, a light-hearted comedy. I went from despicable to hysterical, which basically sums up Hollywood,

In 1985, I traveled to a foreign location for the first time for *Transylvania 6-5000*, shooting in what was then Zagreb, Yugoslavia. Most of the movies we worked on were being done on location, and I was having the time of my life now that I was more comfortable with the demands of a film set.

I interviewed the stars Ed Begley Jr. and Geena Davis (who would later marry her costar Jeff Goldblum). The title *Transylvania 6-5000* is a pun on the song "Pennsylvania 6-5000" made famous by Glenn Miller. The comedy featured Begley and Goldblum as supermarket-tabloid writers in search of a Frankenstein monster that was sighted in a remote European village. I brought my own TV crew and we shot everything we could, not knowing what I would need for the profile. We shot castles, palaces, bustling markets, beautiful flower gardens in the countryside, cobblestone streets, and open horse-drawn carriages.

All of the movies now have behind-the-scenes footage, which you will often see on the extras on a DVD. Being on location was exhilarating, exciting, and exhausting. The days were fourteen to eighteen hours long, and we had to roll with the punches because whatever happened, we had to go along with it. We were not allowed to slow down production of the film to get the footage I needed. I'm not really a drama queen – though my family probably thinks I am – so I did what I was told and still managed be creative.

Also in 1985, I worked on Neil Simon's film *Brighton Beach Memoirs*, starring Matthew Broderick and Blythe Danner, Gwyneth Paltrow's mother. It was exciting and took me to New York. In those days, I brought my own crew because I didn't know that I could just hire a local crew. This was a process, and I was still learning lessons as I went along.

After we did the initial shooting of the behind-the-scenes footage and some of the interviews, we knew we were coming back after going to Europe on location for *Transylvania 6-5000*. *Brighton Beach Memoirs* was a very big movie, which meant many days working on the film set. When we returned to the United States, we shot more of *Brighton Beach Memoirs*. It was really cool to go from one film to another.

My next interview was with Blythe Danner in the kitchen of her home. What a charmer! She is a Tony Award-winning actress who has been around show business for a long time, so she set a very good example for her daughter, Gwyneth, now an Academy Award–winning actress. Blythe is very comfortable with who she is and talked very openly in response to my questions.

My second foreign film set, a few months after *Transylvania 6-5000*, was in France. My husband, who became part of my TV crew as an assistant, went with me for the film, *Flagrant désir* (also released as *Trade Secrets*), starring Sam Waterston, Lauren

Hutton and Marisa Berenson. It was set in the Bordeaux region in the South of France, where the great wines come from. At the lunch break they served not only delicious food and fabulous bread, but also wine; how very French.

The owner of Château Giscours, where we were shooting exteriors, hosted an elegant sit-down dinner party for the film's stars, to which they invited my husband and me and our crew. The appetizers were served in the entry hall, which was bigger than the first floor of my home. They served radishes from their garden and wine from their vineyard. It so impressed me that whenever I have people over for dinner, cocktails served in my living room are always accompanied by a bowl of radishes. A great memory of a wonderful time, and the only film I ever worked on where I was included in the parties. I felt as if I was in the film from the way I was treated.

My life was so exciting and I was so happy with how successful I had become in my career that I thought I was crazy because I couldn't stop eating. Craft service tables, filled with snacks for the crew and cast on a film set, became my typical hangout. The tempting choices included Red Vines licorice (my favorite), pretzels, potato chips, donuts, sweet rolls, and basically anything filled with sugar or salt or fried. Once when I was in a film studio commissary in the South, there wasn't anything that wasn't fried except the cottage cheese; of course, I ate everything.

Nearly Famous

During that time in my life, I never looked at my body, and when I put on my makeup every day, I never acknowledged my double chin or that I had rolls of fat lying on my thighs. If I did, it would make it real and I would have to face that my eating was out of control.

Chapter Ten

In 1985, Universal International gave me the surprise of my life when they hired me to interview film legend Jimmy Stewart for the re-release of *The Glenn Miller Story*, also starring June Allyson. The 1954 film starred Stewart as the swing-era bandleader whose plane disappeared over the English Channel on a trip to entertain the troops in France during World War II. Six decades later, Miller is still listed as "missing in action."

I thought it was just a part of my deal working for the domestic market, but I found out later that this would lead to a new opportunity for me to work on celebrity profiles for the international marketplace in the 90s.

Reba Merrill

I sat down with Jimmy Stewart at his publicist's home in Beverly Hills. The distinguished actor, who was seventy-seven at that time, sat in a wing back chair. He was not acting much anymore because he had lost hearing in one ear, and he was very self-conscious that now he was losing the hearing in the other one. I was told to sit as close as I could so that he could hear me. It was a thrill to sit down with a legend, but when I was given a list of "dos and don'ts", it gave me tension in my neck and made me uncomfortable, which is not how you want to feel when you're doing an interview. Luckily, the minute we started talking, he made me feel so comfortable that I relaxed and enjoyed the experience of a lifetime.

I was told that I had thirty minutes with Mr. Stewart and that I was to call him that, but due to his slow cadence of speech, it turned into ninety minutes of stories about his personal life, his career and his leading ladies.

Mr. Stewart was charming and engaging; he didn't seem to have a problem with the additional time and neither did his publicist, Paul Lindenschmidt.

Before appearing in nearly one hundred films in addition to stage roles and becoming one of the most popular and beloved actors of our time, Stewart struggled as most actors do. In the 1930s, he was living in New York City trying to work on Broadway and was locked out of his hotel room because he didn't have any money. He needed thirty-six dollars, so he called his father to wire it to him. He told me how his father came through and sent the money; then he paused, in a typical James Stewart moment, and said, "And he never let me forget it."

In 1940, Stewart was nominated for an Academy Award along with some of most accomplished actors of that time: Laurence Olivier (*Rebecca*), Raymond Massey (*Abe Lincoln in Illinois*), Henry Fonda (*The Grapes of Wrath*—he was also Stewart's close friend), and Charlie Chaplin (*The Great Dictator*). His film was The Philadelphia Story, which also starred Katharine Hepburn and Cary Grant, and I think in today's Oscar race he would have been nominated as a supporting actor. But despite that formidable competition, James Stewart was awarded the

Oscar for Best Actor. He sent the Oscar to his father in Indiana, Pennsylvania, who set it in his hardware shop where it remained for over twenty years.

He told me he wasn't dating anyone in particular in 1940 and wasn't even planning to attend the Academy Awards until he got a call suggesting that it might be a good idea for him to show up at the Biltmore Hotel for the ceremony. *The Philadelphia Story* was nominated for six awards and, in addition to Stewart's Best Actor Oscar, also won for Best Adapted Screenplay. This was before television, so the Academy Awards ceremony was not seen around the world as it is today, but it was still an important publicity opportunity for the stars. Mr. Stewart told me that he agreed to go because he liked the idea of partying with his friends.

He talked about how glamorous Hollywood was and that he got a crush on most of his leading ladies, including Grace Kelly, Kim Novak, Doris Day, and June Allyson. Always the gentleman, it all sounded perfectly innocent. He was married only once, at the age of forty-one in 1949, to Gloria, the love of his life. When she died in 1994 he stopped making public appearances. They had twin daughters and he adopted Gloria's two sons from a previous marriage. Stewart was one of the first actors to enlist in the US Air Force, retired from the reserves as a brigadier general at the time of the interview.

With his hearing almost gone, the actor who was beloved as "the everyman" and "the ordinary hero" made one of his last public appearances in 1984 when he received the honorary Oscar for Lifetime Achievement. In addition to the 1940 Oscar for Best Actor, he was nominated five times for roles in many classics, including many of Frank Capra's films. Ironically, Cary Grant, who was not nominated for his role in *The Philadelphia Story*, presented the Honorary Oscar.

At the end of the interview, I asked him if he would wish my father a happy birthday.

He turned to the camera and said, "You have a charming, smart daughter and I liked the time we spent together doing this interview." That was the present I gave my father that year for his birthday.

That was one of the last interviews Stewart did because of the loss of his hearing. The time I spent with Mr. Stewart was one of the most incredible experiences of my life. He even signed *The Glenn Miller Story* movie poster, a first for me. I have it hanging in my house along with the letter from Jack Lemmon.

I never expected to meet and feel so comfortable with these film legends. I didn't feel I belonged in their league then, though I do now.

The films just kept coming. When Michele Reese at Universal found people who delivered what she wanted, she took care of them. She hired me next to work on *The Money Pit* with Tom Hanks and Shelley Long. That was an interesting story and a different experience from the other films. All the publicity materials had already been shot for *The Money Pit*; Hanks was heading to a remote part of Israel to work on another film (*Every Time We Say Goodbye*) and wouldn't be able to be hooked up by satellite for the upcoming press junket to promote *The Money Pit*.

The studio decided to call me in so I could interview Tom Hanks before he left to go on location. My interview would be a giveaway to all the journalists interviewing Shelley Long and the film's director Richard Benjamin at the press junket, and would be the only interview available with Tom Hanks for this film. It was early in his career, so he just wore a plaid work shirt and didn't dress up for the interview. He was very candid and funny, though he didn't realize he was being funny.

Tom said, "I look like a squirrel on top of a motorcycle." I didn't know what he meant, but I used it anyway because I thought it showed that he was very open and knew that he did not have classic movie star good looks.

He told me, "I was lucky enough to figure out I couldn't do anything else right around the time they started paying me to act. I had no knowledge of what it was I wanted to do, I was just wandering around. I just wanted to goof off as much as possible. Now I get paid to do that."

He grew up in a family that moved a lot, and he had to take many different jobs before becoming an actor. Tom even worked as a bellhop and carried the bags of many famous people before his big break. Eventually, he was asked to join a small theater group and then came to Hollywood. He was noticed for his talent and versatility, and was cast in a variety of roles. Like Jack Lemmon, he could do drama as well as comedy.

One of his first roles was in a TV series, *Bosom Buddies*. Tom and costar Peter Scolari played guys who lived in a women's hotel dressed in drag so they could save money. That led to his first starring film role in *Splash*, with Daryl Hannah as a mermaid who falls in love with his character. *Splash* was a hit and opened the door for Hanks to become one of the most successful and honored actors of our time.

I was fortunate to interview Tom several times over the years and watch his growth as an actor as well as producer and director. He is one of only nine actors who have two Best Actor Academy Awards and shares the distinction with only Spencer Tracy of winning two consecutive Oscars, for *The Philadelphia Story* (1993) and *Forrest Gump* (1994).

I asked him, "You've had a successful career, but not all your movies have worked. How do you deal with that part of it?"

He said, "I have been lucky that the first movie I did was very well received. I've always known that it will be up and down. I think the secret is not to celebrate the highs too much because if you do, then when the inevitable lows come around, and they do, you are going to be lower than you even feel. Because I know sooner or later I am going to try to do something and it is not going to work. And the question I will try to have to answer then is, 'What went wrong? Why in the world would you choose to do something like this? Something that turned out so badly?' So I think the secret is to make sure you are doing it because you love the material no matter what. It is going to be fun for you, no matter what. And then if it's successful, it is an added bonus. But if it is not successful, they still can't take away the experience."

In one of our later interviews, I mentioned that I had interviewed Jimmy Stewart, which caught his attention. I could tell he was much more impressed with me than he was at our first interview for *The Money Pit*. He has been called another

Jimmy Stewart. Like Jimmy and Gloria Stewart, Tom and actress/producer Rita Wilson have one of the most successful marriages in Hollywood. They first met when Rita was a guest on *Bosom Buddies* and then started a relationship when they costarred together in the film *Volunteers*; they were married in 1988 and now have two sons.

I asked him, as I had Jimmy Stewart, how he would like to be remembered: as a movie star or an actor?

He said, "I know I'm a movie star. I would much rather be known as being an actor…I would be very happy if people, years from now, are looking at my performance and saying, 'Man, that guy could do anything.' That would really make me happy."

Like Tom Hanks, I didn't know what I wanted to do. Then I started doing celebrity interviews, and I finally realized I was a journalist, and that the studios were willing to pay me for it.

Chapter Eleven

In 1986 I did an electronic press kit, or EPK, for a movie called *8 Million Ways to Die*. Eddie Kalish from Producers Sales Organization hired me, even though TriStar would eventually distribute the film. We were filming in a Malibu castle, which had an outside slanted elevator that took us to the front door and down to the courtyard. The movie starred Jeff Bridges and Patricia Arquette. More important than the stars of the film was the director, Hal Ashby. Probably one of the most famous directors in Hollywood, Ashby was known for the cult classic *Harold and Maude* as well as for many other films, including *The Last Detail*, *Shampoo*, *Coming Home*, and *Being There*. This would be his last feature film.

I had never worked on a film set where drugs were so prevalent and the director was high through most of the shoot. He threw me off the set a few times, then sometimes he didn't know who I was or why I was there. Needless to say, it was both exciting and frustrating.

Jeff Bridges talked about getting acting jobs on his father's TV show, *Sea Hunt*, when he was only eight years old. He told me that he liked roles that "scare the hell out of me. I'm not sure that I can pull it off. It's not a bad thing to feel fear, but what you have to do is go there. That's how you get rid of it."

Jeff kept a photographic journal of all his films and sometimes turned them into books. His mother made a photo album for him and each of his siblings: his brother, actor Beau Bridges, and their sister, Lucinda. This so impressed me that my husband and I made albums for each of our children.

One funny moment occurred because I was wearing a retainer. While interviewing Jeff my tongue was slipping on the roof of my mouth, and I couldn't get the words out. I said, "Excuse me, I have to take this retainer out."

He started to laugh and said, "You remind me of my wife. She wears one, too." That really broke the ice.

I have interviewed Jeff quite a few times, and every time was a pleasure. He is a gentleman, gracious, and, most importantly, he knows that my job is to sell the movie and that his job is to help me. When I saw him in *Crazy Heart*, I knew he was going to win an Oscar for that performance, and he did in 2009.

Andy Garcia also starred in *8 Million Ways to Die*. I was told to do his interview in Spanish; I don't speak Spanish. We compromised. I asked him the questions in English and he answered me in Spanish. I had no idea what he was saying, so somebody else had to edit the piece. I had to follow the same procedure for the film *Shattered*, directed by Wolfgang Petersen. I asked the questions in English, he answered in German, and somebody else had to cut it. When I was hired for a film and they asked me to do something, I had learned that it was best to just do it and never question what I was asked to do.

I also did video profiles for *Soul Man* with James Earl Jones, *Avenging Angels*, *Flowers in the Attic*, *Heathers*, and *Girls Just Want to Have Fun*. These New World films were smaller, with less pressure and more opportunity for me. During that time I interviewed Sarah Jessica Parker, Helen Hunt, and Winona Ryder, three young actresses at the beginning of their careers. We were all just starting out.

While I was working for Bill Shields at New World, he took me over to meet Robert Shaye, president of New Line Cinema. They are now known for producing the very successful *The Lord of the Rings* trilogy, which won seventeen of its thirty Oscar nominations, and are releasing two films based on *The Hobbit* in 2012 and 2013. At that time, in 1987, they were doing movies like *Nightmare on Elm Street*. In fact, the first film role Johnny Depp ever got was a small role in *Nightmare on Elm Street*, and he later told me that he was paid "the most money he had ever seen in his life." Depp was a musician in a garage band and nobody hired him for his music, but that's another story that I'll tell you later.

Robert Shaye hired me for *Nightmare on Elm Street 3*. I decided after looking at the film, and watching Robert Englund work, that I didn't want to dilute the power of the character. Freddy Krueger was more famous than the actor who played him, so we decided to interview Freddy instead of Robert. We were able to videotape him as he was shot in the film, in makeup and with the right lighting. I shot the behind-the-scenes footage in such a way that you could not see him without makeup, creating the illusion that I was actually sitting down with the real Freddy Krueger. It was a lot of fun because Englund was very talented and convincing in the role.

When an actor has a good time making a film, it makes the interview so much more enjoyable. He joked that he had his nails done as Freddy Krueger at the same place I had mine done. I didn't use that comment in the interview, but it was kind of a nice icebreaker! We really hit it off. Robert Englund even invited me to his wedding reception, which my husband and I attended when he married his wife Nancy in 1988. They are still married over twenty-three years later, a long time by Hollywood standards.

Some of the actors from the various *Nightmare on Elm Street* films became very famous. Robert Englund went on to do other things just like I did. A lot of young actors, including Johnny Depp and Patricia Arquette, and also young directors, like Renny Harlin who later did *Die Hard 2*, get their start in films from companies like New World and New Line; the smaller studios have their place in Hollywood. I'm really glad that I was part of that.

Surprisingly, I didn't know how much I was a part of it until I looked back at the interviews. At the time, none of these people meant anything to me, because they were totally unknown and, for many, this was their first movie. When I sat down with them again years later, they would say: "Oh, I remember you. You did this film with me."

I worked with New Line consistently and was even given Christmas presents. As a vendor I was supposed to give them Christmas presents but they gave me gifts, and they even invited me to their Christmas parties. I produced publicity materials for their films from 1984 until 1988 and really felt like a part of the family.

Chapter Twelve

In 1987, I went on location to upstate New York for the film *Ironweed*, which would be Oscar-nominated in 1988 against *Rain Man*. I knew that I would not be allowed to interview or shoot behind-the-scenes footage of Jack Nicholson. That left me with his costar, Meryl Streep. I shot footage of Jack working, but no one knew because I had my cameraman turn his light off. Jack joked around with the TV crew and me as long as the camera was not running. Meryl Streep, on the other hand, let us shoot behind-the-scenes footage of her. The film's unit publicist arranged Meryl's interview, and when the scheduled time came, we were set up and ready.

What a surprise when Meryl arrived with wet hair, glasses, and no make up. No had one told her that this was a video interview, not print. I told her, "This interview will last a long time, and I don't think you want to look that way on video." I left the film set with all the interviews except the one with the star of the film. When I came back to Los Angeles, I told the producers I did not have Meryl's interview.

I was sent back to New York to interview Meryl, where I picked up a crew and met her at a hotel on Madison Avenue. When I returned to do the interview, she was comfortable with me. Maybe it was because she saw me often during the three-week period on the film; maybe it was because I had been honest with her and said, "Please don't do the interview with wet hair and no makeup and glasses."

For our next interview, the studio provided Meryl with her personal hair and makeup person at the cost of $1,500. About a third of the way through the interview, she put her hand through her hair and got it all messed up, undoing the work of her expensive stylist. The same stylist, J. Roy Helland, won an Oscar in the Hair and Makeup category for turning Meryl into Margaret Thatcher in The Iron Lady. When he accepted his Oscar, he thanked Meryl for keeping him employed for over 30 years.

Reba Merrill

Meryl gave me a very revealing, hour-long interview about the woman she was, what made her tick, and what was important in her life. "I still get nervous, very nervous, when I have to audition," she told me, which is probably not something she has to do anymore since she is considered one of the most talented and respected actresses of our time. The most candid moment of our interview was when she told me that she could not ask her housekeeper to remove the dust balls in the closet.

In addition to numerous other entertainment awards, she has been nominated for an Academy Award a record seventeen times and has won three: Best Supporting Actress for *Kramer vs. Kramer* and Best Actress for *Sophie's Choice* and for *The Iron Lady*. In her acceptance speech at the 2012 Oscars for playing Margaret Thatcher, she thanked Roy Helland and congratulated him on winning an Oscar. Katharine Hepburn is the only actress to have won four Oscars and no other actress besides Meryl has won three.

Meryl became interested in acting at Vassar and then headed to the prestigious Yale School of Drama. "I decided to be an actress halfway through drama school. It was something that was hard to commit to because I didn't think it was a serious sort of way to spend your life. Or one that would help the world… But now I think my mind has changed about that. It is a valuable thing."

It was one of those magical times when the star was comfortable enough to be candid. It surprised me when she said, "If I have to sing in front of people, I am just terrified," though she had taken voice lessons for years. She sang in *Ironwood* and in a few of her other films, including in *Silkwood*, *Postcards from the Edge*, and later in *Mamma Mia*.

"I had a lot of breaks early on." Meryl, who is extremely shy, told me that when her entire drama class prepared and was invited to audition for Joe Papp's Public Theater, "I was too nervous, I couldn't go. But basically I didn't want to be a part of that whole 'meat market.' Competition makes me very nervous. The next day I went to the woman who arranged the auditions and said, 'Give me a chance to read for it.' And she did and I don't know why. She was just a nice woman." She got an audition with Joe Papp, who cast her in *Trelawny of the Wells*, which was her Broadway debut at Lincoln Center in 1975.

Since then, she has appeared in over fifty films, making her movie debut in *Julia* with Jane Fonda and Vanessa Redgrave in 1977 and earning her first Oscar nomination in 1978 for *The Deer Hunter*. "I know a lot of my success has to do with luck. I've also poured a lot of hard work into it, so I feel that in some way, I can justify myself. I am just happy that life has happened this way."

The most candid moment of our interview was when she told me that she could not ask her housekeeper to remove the dust balls in the closet.

She has been married since 1978. "The greatest break in my life is when I met Don Gummer. There is no question in my mind about that." Meryl and her husband, a well-known sculptor, have four children, three girls and a boy. Her two oldest daughters, Mamie and Grace, are both actresses and look just like Meryl did when she first started her career.

She described perfectly how so many actors feel, and how they hate having to do interviews like this to promote their films: "I am much more comfortable enclosed in a world of fiction."

I was in awe of this extraordinary woman, who was as kind and humble as she is talented. "I never imagined in my wildest dreams that I would be successful. The fear is always there for an actress that you will never work again. That goes with the territory…so each happy event as it has happened has been a surprise."

After the interview, Meryl told me that she would be leaving the country for *A Cry in the Dark*, which would put her in Australia when the publicity for *Ironweed* was to be released. I offered to make her a video of the sound bites used in the profile and send her a transcript. All she had to do was to strike out what she didn't want used. She sent us back the edited transcript and went to Australia. As the release date of the film got closer, a consultant hired by the production company called me. I was told to turn over Meryl Streep's interview to be edited by the man who hit on me for sex at Fox years earlier. The old boys' network kept getting him jobs even though he lost his big position at Fox after being charged with sexual harassment by a woman at the studio, and his career came tumbling down. I told him that I could only turn over the approved footage, nothing else. I even got my lawyer involved.

The end result was that I kept my word to Meryl, and he got the pleasure of threatening me with the famous Hollywood line: "You will never work in this town again." It didn't work this time either. I never had to turn over the interview footage, we edited the Meryl Streep profile, and I worked in Hollywood for another twenty years.

Chapter Thirteen

The movies kept coming, and I added TriStar as a client. I was hired for a lot of EPK's in 1986 and 1987, including TriStar's *Like Father Like Son*, starring Dudley Moore and Kurt Cameron as a father and son who switched places. Also in 1987, I worked on *Blind Date*, which gave me a chance to sit down with Kim Basinger in her publicist's office. Kim came from a little town in Georgia and had studied ballet from the age of three. In addition to her film roles, she had appeared in hundreds of ads and was one of the Breck Shampoo Girls. I don't think she enjoyed doing the interview. She was professional but stiff and didn't seem comfortable in her own skin. When I kept saying how nice these people were to me, a studio executive told me, "They will take it out on us. They always are nice to the press." For some reason, the actors thought I was the press, even though I worked for the studio.

There were a lot of actors who went out of their way to be cooperative, taking time between shots to meet with me, like Arnold Schwarzenegger, whom I met when he starred in *Running Man*. I was hired by the production company, Keith Barish Productions, and not TriStar, the studio that distributed the film. One of the things that jumped out at me from the Schwarzenegger interview was when I asked him what was the best thing he had ever done. I thought he was going to say either his movies or his bodybuilding career.

He replied, "The best thing that I ever did was to become an American citizen." I never forgot that, and it certainly proved to be a good decision when he later ran for governor of California and served two terms.

In the mid-eighties, women were starting to get more power in the marketing divisions of studios, big and small. First, women took over publicity, then advertising, and eventually the whole marketing division. I didn't realize that as more and more women got a foothold in the marketing divisions, I would get less and less work. Once they had made it big, women in Hollywood frequently did not want competition from anyone else. Worst of all, they could get away with their bitchiness as long as some powerful man protected them. There was no way somebody like me, an outside vendor, could get work if the female executive had a powerful studio boss behind her. It not only affected me, but also other women who were considered a threat. It's still happening today.

Why is it that some women feel so threatened by other women? I like to reach out and mentor young women who are just starting out in publicity and teach them what I learned along the way. Whenever I give speeches to women working in the film industry, I let them know what's involved and offer to help where I can. I'm hoping that today, in this new millennium, women are paving the way for other women and do not feel threatened by a woman who simply does a good job.

Michele Reese left Universal and was hired by De Laurentis Entertainment, where we would continue to work together. She said that what I did for her, producing celebrity profiles that the TV stations wanted to air, took one thing off her shoulders that she didn't have to worry about. Even with Michele gone, I kept getting hired by Universal until I made a big mistake. On every film I would interview the stars, the producer, the costumer, and, of course, the director. On *Biloxi Blues*, part of the Neil Simon trilogy, I was thrilled to sit down with Neil in his Beverly Hills home and found him to be literate, charming, and a good storyteller.

I went to New York to finish shooting behind-the-scenes for the film footage and to interview the film's director Mike Nichols, who won an Oscar for *The Graduate*. He felt that his interview was too candid and would not let me produce a profile on him, even though he had signed a release. I believe that his comments about the interview, made to the insecure woman who hired me, made her feel that it was easier to throw me under the bus than to stand up for me.

Maybe I am being too hard on a studio executive who loved the power she had and would go to any lengths to keep it. She could do whatever she wanted since she was protected by her boss for many reasons. One of the rumors I heard was that they were very close. To protect the guilty, they will remain nameless. After Biloxi Blues, she never hired me again. When a whole studio fired me, it became the biggest and most painful lesson I learned.

Of all the lessons I was trying to learn, this was one I hadn't picked up yet, and it really hit hard. I only worked on one more film for Universal, for the International Division nearly a decade later. It wasn't until 1991 that I learned not to question what the client wanted. I have to say this: most of the people who know what they're doing listen to the people they've hired. The studio executives that don't know what they're doing insist on putting their stamp on the work, thinking that will make it right, and then it doesn't work. I met more and more people like that, and it was a lesson that took me a long time to learn.

Biloxi Blues was my swan song for Universal, and I thought that it was going to be the swan song for my whole career. Luckily, it turned out that it wasn't. When I look back on my career, the most amazing movies I worked with came after leaving Universal. At De Laurentis Entertainment Group, Michele was given a bigger title and more power. She was now second in command to Edward Roginski, who was now the president of marketing. I absolutely adored working for Ed Roginski, one of the most brilliant marketing minds around. When he died of AIDS at the age of forty-four in 1988, I was so devastated that I actually did something I had never done before nor have since. I wrote a letter to *Variety*, the entertainment industry trade paper, saying he was a man who loved movies and that I loved working for him. He was an extraordinary man, and working for him was an exciting learning experience. Even though I was an outside vendor, Ed made me feel like a part of the team, and showed his respect for my work by giving me interesting films to work on and allowing me to be creative.

That year, I was hired for the film *Torch Song Trilogy*, right after my mother died. I had only been home a few days after her funeral in Denver when I realized this was the second time I was interviewing Anne Bancroft in a little over a year. I was the heaviest I had ever been, tipping the scales at 209 pounds. I had added an extra ten to fifteen pounds during my time bonding with my mother, who had spent her last days eating junk food.

Anne still remembered me from our interview for *'night, Mother* for Universal the year before. Anne was the mother and Sissy Spacek played the daughter in the film version of the Pulitzer Prize-winning Broadway play that dealt with the subject of suicide. After the film wrapped, Anne threw a party for everybody who worked on *'night, Mother*, and my crew and I were included. We made a video to play at the party, a spoof we called *Little Night Mother*. It was an interesting evening because Mel Brooks was there. He played second fiddle to his wife, Anne, because it was her night, her film, and her party. I was pleasantly surprised because Mel was the more famous of the two in that marriage.

She was born Anna Maria Italiano to middle-class parents who lived in the Bronx. Her mother dreamed of her young daughter being an actress. Anne told me, "She dreamt it so hard that I thought it was my dream and I accepted that dream... From the time I could talk, I sang, and from the time that I could walk, I danced."

The Hollywood studios did not want her to have such an ethnic name, so she chose Bancroft because it sounded so terribly English. Michael Caine, born Maurice Joseph Micklewhite, did the same thing since he was English and he wanted a name that sounded very proper. Today, most actors keep their names, even if they don't sound like they should be on a marquee.

Anne Bancroft burst onto Hollywood in 1952 under contract and appeared in one movie after another. All of the sudden, about four years later, everything fell apart. Her first marriage ended and she was being cast only in B movies. She thought her film career was over, so she went to New York and auditioned for roles in theater. She starred in *Two for the Seesaw* and won a Tony. She played Anne Sullivan in *The Miracle Worker* and won another Tony. In 1962, she won the Oscar for Best Actress for reprising that role in the film of the same name, which brought her back to Hollywood. She never left.

Nearly Famous

In 1961, she had met Mel Brooks at a rehearsal for *The Perry Como Show*. Bancroft was performing a song called "Married, I Could Always Get." After she finished singing, she was greeted by Brooks who proclaimed, "I'm Mel Brooks and I'm going to marry you."

In our interview, Anne told me that after meeting Mel, "I went to my psychiatrist at that time and I said, 'Come on, let's hurry this up. I met the guy, I want to be all ready and healthy, and I want this one to last.'" They were married in 1964.

She was one of the very few actresses who have won a Tony, an Emmy and an Oscar, yet she still felt insecure about her talent. "With almost everything I do, I think 'Oh God, I can't do this'... but I love to see if it is going to stretch me, if it is going to make me dig into pockets of myself that I haven't been into for a long time."

She played Mrs. Robinson in *The Graduate* in 1967. She was only six years older than her costar Dustin Hoffman, who played the young man right out of college whom she seduces.

In 1972, she played Winston Churchill's mother, the American-born Jenny Jerome, in a movie called *Young Winston*. While they were shooting the film, the former Prime Minister came onto the set, and when he saw how much Anne, in hair and makeup, looked like his mother, he cried.

What was interesting and amazing about Anne's marriage to Mel is that they made it work. If Mel was working, she made sure that she wasn't, so she could be with him. When their only son Max was born, she knew that she had to be home to take care of him. She said about Mel, "We are very much in sync and deep down, not on a show- business level but on a deep gut level, we agree on what life is about."

For their twenty-first wedding anniversary, Mel bought Anne the rights to the film *84 Charing Cross Road*. He produced it and she starred in it. He was quoted as saying that from the day they met, February 5, 1961, they were glued together. Mel Brooks made audiences laugh and Anne Bancroft made him smile. They were married forty-one years when she died on June 6, 2005 from uterine cancer. She lived long enough to see her first grandson, who was born two months before she passed away. One of the things she said about her relationship with her husband was, "Life was not measured by the number of breaths one took, but by the number of moments that took one's breath away."

Anne Bancroft was an extraordinary woman who treated me with great respect. My experience of meeting her would come full circle in an unexpected way over twenty years later. In 2011, I went to the memorial for former studio head John Calley on a soundstage on the Sony lot. I had worked on a couple of John's movies when he was president of Sony Pictures. Hundreds of his friends and colleagues attended the service, including Mel Brooks. After the tributes, we were all invited to the other side of the soundstage, where they had set up a beautiful candlelit restaurant serving all the foods that John Calley had loved.

As I was walking into the reception, I ended up right behind Mel Brooks. I put my arm on his shoulder and said I had had the pleasure of interviewing Anne to promote a couple of her movies. He pulled me aside and asked, "Which movies?"

I said that one was 'night Mother, and that I knew this was a film that had challenged her and how proud she was of it. He kissed me on the cheek. The other was *Torch Song Trilogy*, the film I was working on after my mother passed away.

I told him, "When I went on the set and told your wife that my mother had recently died, Anne decided to cheer me up and said, 'Can I tell you a story about my husband? When I met him, I said to myself, What more could you want? He looks like my father, acts like my mother. I'll have everything I've ever felt safe with.'"

His eyes filled with tears as he said – and not in a funny Mel Brooks voice— "Thank you." For that moment, he wasn't Mel Brooks the comedian saying, "Thank you." He was the man, Mel Brooks, who loved his wife.

Chapter Fourteen

Judi Schwam, senior vice president of Worldwide Publicity and Promotion at United Artists, asked me to interview Diane Keaton for the film, *Baby Boom*. They finished shooting the film, and all the materials for the electronic press kit were done except for the star Diane Keaton's interview. The crew shooting behind-the-scenes footage didn't get an interview with her. Another company was hired just to do Diane's interview, but the studio didn't like it. A hotel room was booked, and hair and makeup people and a TV crew were hired to do just that one interview.

When I asked Diane about her childhood, she told me that she knew she wanted to perform at about the age of five, and both of her parents "were very encouraging to me, always... My father in particular was always really thrilled when I would be on stage. That was very rewarding when Daddy likes you," she said as she laughed.

"The thing was, it was like a blank slate in here [pointing to her head], I didn't know what it would be. I still don't know what is coming up. And I don't think you ever are really prepared for any of it."

Diane began her career on stage as a member of the "Tribe" and the understudy to Sheila in the original Broadway production of *Hair*. She gained some notoriety for her refusal to disrobe at the end of Act I when the cast performs nude; even though nudity in the production was optional for actors, those who performed nude received a $50 bonus. Later in her career, she got to sing again in the film *Looking for Mr. Goodbar* with Richard Gere.

When I asked her about fame, she said, "No, no, no, it couldn't be what you think it is. It is just ridiculous. Fame is much more interesting and complicated and all those things, but ultimately I really feel if you can survive fame and kind of have your feet on the ground, still, then you've done something pretty good. Because I don't think it is easy."

She told me that she got very nervous trying out for a role. "I was not very good at auditioning...I think you have elements of all the people you play somewhere in you. They are always sort of lurking about…I look for one thing, one thing only: is it a good script? Do I have a feeling for it? That's all I am looking for."

She won an Academy Award for *Annie Hall*. "The thing about the Oscar is that I don't remember a thing about it. It was gone. All I remember is driving on the freeway the next morning to my parents' house thinking that it had happened but what was it? I didn't know. I was a little excited about it."

Woody Allen, her lover at the time who wrote and directed the film, named it after her, and it is thought to be about their relationship. Hall is her real last name and Annie was her nickname. She changed her last name to her mother's maiden name because there was a Diane Hall already in the Actors Guild. The masculine-style clothes she wore in the film, which is now considered a classic, were her own and started a trend. I was surprised to learn that her films have earned over $1.1 billion at the box office, which few actresses have achieved. In addition to acting, Diane is also a photographer and a real-estate developer, still sings occasionally, appears in L'Oréal ads, and is a spokeswoman for Chico's.

What I remember most about my first interview with Diane Keaton is the studio executive Judi Schwam sitting on the floor smiling to stay out of the shot; she knew we got what she was looking for with this interview. I cut four profiles with the footage we shot, each focusing on a different topic that we had discussed. I interviewed Diane again almost eight years later for *Father of the Bride II*.

At the age of fifty, she adopted her daughter Dexter and five years later, her son Duke, although she has never married. One thing I did not do was ask her about her leading men and the relationships she had with them. In addition to Woody Allen, she was linked with some of her other costars, including Warren Beatty and Al Pacino. Private life is private, unless the star brings it up. However, she did say that if she hadn't had a successful career, "I don't know what my life would have been like. I can only imagine that I would have been a miserable, unhappy person, an undeveloped, ignorant woman who was driving some poor guy nuts because I was so emotional."

When I was writing this book, Diane Keaton admitted in her just-published autobiography, *Then Again*, that she suffered from bulimia, which had started, during her relationship with Allen when she was in her twenties. She never talked about having an eating disorder with me and it is something I would never have asked her, although she may have sensed something in that interview that was unspoken and understood the shame I was experiencing as a compulsive overeater. I was wearing a tight size 16— working my way to an 18— and could not hide my weight, even though I thought I knew how to dress to hide my belly that was lying on my thighs.

Emotional eating defined me and drove me to who I had become, as well as the way I acted in business and with my family. At the time, I didn't know if I was strong enough to let go of the sugar that controlled my life for over seven years. As addicts often do, I kept my compulsive eating a secret. I would hide candy in my pockets or better yet "palm it" so no one, especially my husband, would see what I was going to eat. I often ate in the car, always getting rid of the wrappers, containers and the smell, keeping an air freshener handy.

I never asked myself, "Why can't I stop?" I didn't know I was an addict because it was only candy, not alcohol or drugs. I didn't even know there was a twelve-step program that could help me. When I went to my first Overeaters Anonymous meeting, I discovered that I was not alone and met people who were addicted just like me; I found out they could give up sugar and white flour, which turns into sugar. That's what it was about for me: finding out I wasn't crazy and learning the steps for a better, healthier, and thinner life.

Looking back, I am surprised that I had a big, successful career because I was living day-to-day addicted to sugar. I felt sorry for myself, even though I was sitting in my beautiful home in Malibu on the beach and drove a red convertible that was paid off., I still felt that I never had enough. To feed my addiction and soothe the fear, I filled produce bags with cheap chocolate-covered peanuts from the bin in the grocery store and ate the candy all at night when I was alone until I passed out. I hid the candy and my addictive behavior from my husband, who told me he didn't see the extra weight since he is the kind of man who looks at his wife through eyes of love.

I only realized while working on this book that food was my friend when I was happy, scared, sad, or angry, and that compulsive eating really had nothing to do with being hungry. Food was always there for me and never judged me. I had experienced so much rejection in the past; I had been let go from four talk shows and had no job offers despite all the networking and applying for TV shows around the country. When I started producing video publicity, I kept getting more and more work from the studios and received so many accolades that I never realized I had a fear of failure. I just kept eating to avoid my feelings, while telling myself the lie that I was a victim and with all the extra weight, "No one will ever hit on me again." Another realization has been that since the fat Fox executive was someone to conveniently blame for my overeating, I never had to look at what was really going on inside of me.

The truth was, I wasn't happy despite all the material trappings. Something was missing from my life, and I realize now I didn't feel worthy or deserving of my success.

Could the little girl who was raised to only marry well and be taken care of really have "made it" in Hollywood? I would never admit to myself or to anyone else, until now, that I was afraid it was too much too soon, and that it was all a fluke that could end at any moment.

I realized my insecurities affected my attitude and behavior toward others. The incompetence of some of the people at the studios and mean-spirited publicists provoked me to anger, and I took it out on the people I worked closely with on my staff—including my daughter, who was my editor. I realize now that the rage also came from my body not metabolizing the sugar that turned me into a bitch. I felt that I was going crazy because I could not control my eating, emotions and actions.

In the mid-eighties, when my income started to soar, I wrongly and unfairly fired someone who had all the attributes

Nearly Famous

I wanted: she was educated, accomplished in her career, a good writer, nice to work with, and, most importantly, she was thin! I couldn't have imagined, and neither could she, that twenty-five years later she would be the co-writer of this book, and the writing process would turn into a therapy session where I discovered my jealousy of her.

Before I hired her, she had been a journalist who interviewed celebrities. In my insecurity, I feared that if the studios found out about her background, they would want her instead of me. It was easier to fire her and make sure that wouldn't happen, while I covered up my self-doubt by feeding my addiction with sugar. Looking back, it was probably a blessing that when I was overdosing on sugar, I didn't remember all my bad behavior. Thankfully, even now, I only remember some of it.

Chapter Fifteen

After the interview went so well with Diane Keaton, Judi Schwam hired me for *Rain Man*. I planned to go on the set and shoot behind-the-scenes footage in hopes of picking up the interviews with the stars, Dustin Hoffman and Tom Cruise.

Then I found out that Cruise was really uncomfortable having a TV crew around, so the set was closed. We had no behind-the-scenes footage and couldn't do the interviews until they set them up long after the production wrapped. The film was going to be released in December and I did the interviews in September, 1988, so that gave us a lot of time to produce the video profiles – I just didn't have all the elements. I met with Tom Cruise and Dustin Hoffman separately, and then interviewed executive producers Peter Guber and Jon Peters, the director Barry Levinson, and the producer Mark Johnson.

I didn't know what to expect when I sat down with Dustin first. He was very funny and he liked making me laugh, so the interview took a long time because I kept taking bathroom breaks: I thought I was going to explode! The more I laughed, the more it encouraged him to say outrageous things. He was extremely comfortable telling me all kinds of stories,

especially about the early days when he couldn't find work in show business. He told me that he went to Santa Monica City College because "I didn't have the grades to get into a university. So they said 'take an acting class, it's an easy three credits' and I just loved it."

He left there and went to Pasadena Playhouse, where he became friends with Gene Hackman. Their classmates voted them "Least Likely to Succeed." He said, "It was even more a joke that we got anywhere because we never expected to."

When Dustin went to New York, he moved in with Gene and took all kinds of jobs to survive. Dustin begged Gene to let him work with him at a moving company because he made such good money. "Finally, he said I could work for one day, and

I realized that all his jobs were tenements with no elevators. I carried a couple of boxes of books, and after a few hours, I said goodbye."

Despite the hardships, he said one of the things that kept him going was, " I loved being with actors, hanging out with them. There was a family there that I had not experienced before, and if I really had to go into it I would have to say I didn't become an actor to be an actor— I became an actor to find a family." He continued to study acting at the Actors Studio and starred off-Broadway to critical acclaim in the play *Eh?*

"If we could have made a living getting some nice parts off-Broadway for the rest of our lives, we would have been quite content and I would have made a pact with the Theater Devil."

"I wanted to be a leading man, but when you get to New York, they tell you what you are. They told me, 'You are a character juvenile.' That means you play the funny-looking guy to the good-looking lead. When Mike Nichols cast me in *The Graduate*, I was the first to tell him I was not right for that part. I think Robert Redford tested for it the day before, who was perfect for it, at least physically."

After Dustin auditioned, Nichols called him up a few days later and said, "You looked really panicked in the screen test, but that is kind of what I want," and he gave him the part. He was thirty years old when he got the role of Benjamin Braddock, but he looked eighteen. This was the beginning of an extraordinary career filled with great roles and not-so-great roles. In fact, he starred in one of the famously worst movies ever made, Ishtar, but that's another story.

He was nominated for an Academy Award for Best Actor for *The Graduate*, the first of his seven nominations to date, and won Best Actor Oscars for *Kramer vs. Kramer* and *Rain Man*. He's the only actor to have top billing in three films that won Best Picture Oscars: *Midnight Cowboy*, *Kramer vs. Kramer* and *Rain Man*.

When I asked Dustin what he would have done if he had not found acting, he said he would've ended up like Ratzo Rizzo, the homeless man he played in *Midnight Cowboy*. He wanted to be a jazz pianist but said he wasn't good enough—although you got to see some of his musical talent when he starred opposite Emma Thompson in *Last Chance Harvey* in 2008.

Humor was his drive. I got a sense of that when he told me a story that I couldn't use when I produced the video profile, but I'm sure I can tell you now. In order to ease the tension during a nude scene with Jane Alexander in *Kramer vs. Kramer*, he wore an orange jockstrap with feathers on it and danced around the room with the cameras rolling. I hope you get an idea of how willing he is to do anything to be funny. I will never forget telling me stories and watching me fall apart. The more I lost it, the more outrageous he became. The only other person that could do that to me was Robin Williams, who couldn't wait to see me crack up.

I asked Dustin how he dealt with a lack of privacy: did he use disguises or did he just not go out? "One of the best disguises I've ever had in my life was Tom Cruise because when we were making *Rain Man*, nobody looked at me. Nobody recognized me. It was wonderful…So I know now if I ever want to walk down the street and never be bothered, I just call up Tom and say, 'Take a walk with me.'"

I called this book *Nearly Famous* because I never reached the level of fame of most of the people I interviewed, so I didn't have to worry about my privacy or being recognized. I did relate to Dustin saying he liked "hanging out" with actors. The time I spent on location and interviewing actors was the most fun I ever had in my life.

My interview with Tom Cruise didn't leave as big of an impression on me, although he was as charming as Dustin was funny. It was before Tom was into Scientology, and I remember he was very shy and charismatic. I asked Tom if he was afraid to take risks. He told me, "I found that when I really loved something that I just went after it ferociously. And every film I do, you get new tools to work with. With each picture, I want to try something new, try something different, you can't be afraid to be humiliated, I want that excitement. I want to get up in the

Nearly Famous

morning and feel those butterflies and know I am not doing the same thing...It's exciting."

Although I wouldn't think I had much in common with Tom Cruise, I also felt, as he did, that I went after my career "ferociously." Instead of giving up when I wasn't being hired for on-camera jobs, I tried something different that turned out to be even more exciting and found that the best was yet to come.

When I sent in the script for the video profile, Tom's personal publicist at that time said, "This is crap—it sounds just like *Entertainment Tonight*." I thought it was the best compliment they could pay because that meant it looked like real TV. All the TV stations played my Cruise interview, including HBO, where it aired continuously for six weeks. If you want to see my interviews with Hoffman and Cruise, they are on the re-mastered DVD of *Rain Man*. In addition to Dustin's Best Actor Oscar, *Rain Man* won an Academy Award for Best Picture, and both men went on to have amazing careers.

Chapter Sixteen

This is probably the hardest thing I've had to talk about. After the fat executive propositioned me, I connected my overeating to the fear of being hit on for work because I didn't know how to deal with it. I was lucky; the man from Fox was so despicable that the decision was made for me. I really don't know what I would have done if he had been good-looking and charming. Fortunately, it was a decision I never had to face.

What I don't understand is why I had to resort to huge amounts of sugar to avoid facing my fear of rejection and failure. I didn't realize that I was fragile and scared, and did not know how to deal with my feelings. Looking back, I can't believe how driven I was to numb myself to cover up my feelings for all these years. I have to admit that somewhere within me, I was always an addict and just didn't know it, or somehow I controlled it. When my addiction took over, I was out of control. It wasn't just that I started to put on weight, which you see in the pictures with Jack Lemmon and Jimmy Stewart; my public behavior started to change. Maybe I was always mean, angry, jealous and filled with rage, and it just never came out of me. I was having so much fun doing what I loved, interviewing movie stars, and yet felt so much rage inside that I took it out on people.

I'm amazed that I had a successful career because my behavior was so destructive. Those closest to me saw the anger, yet no one knew it came from the jealousy I felt toward others who always seemed to have more than I did. Despite what I did have, it was never enough.

On the surface, I appeared to be a highly successful businesswoman with my own company who loved what she was doing, but within me was a fear that it would all be taken away, which manifested in temperamental outbursts.

I put on so much weight that my thighs used to rub together, and I had to wear an undergarment that kept them from actually bleeding. I put makeup on every day and never seemed to notice that I had more than one chin. The secret, I told myself, was that nobody could tell I was fat because I knew how to dress to hide my big belly.

I was being difficult with studio executives who could find ten other people to do what I was doing at that time. The fear that I had been living with was starting to manifest itself with my business slowing down and my income decreasing. Since I wanted the money I had earned to be mine, it caused problems in my marriage and we started talking about the possibility of a divorce. I felt entitled since I had been denied success for so many years and I resented that I lived in a community property state that gave my husband half of everything I earned. It still never occurred to me that I might be causing all of this with my addicted behavior. Going to therapy helped me see that "me" was really only one part of us.

How I got to my first OA meeting is a story filled with drama, which seems to be typical in my life. In 1989, I was hired for the film *Amazon*, to be shot on location in a small village in the jungles of Brazil. You can see in the picture of me interviewing

Rae Dawn Chong how fat I was at that time, with my backside hanging over the stool. I said to the unit publicist working on the film that she looked good and asked how she stayed so thin. She

told me she went to this twelve-step program for food addiction. I have to tell you that my response was not positive because I don't like to drink, and my opinion of women in twelve-step programs was that they must be tramps that were drinking or doing drugs. I was only eating a lot of food and I could go on a diet.

I knew how to diet—after all, I had lost weight for my daughter Cheryl's wedding the year before and gotten down to 185 pounds with Jenny Craig's help. Cheryl and I went shopping for a dress and I was crying. When she asked me why, I said it was because my mother wouldn't be at the wedding.

She replied, "That's not true, you're too fat and can't get into anything." I put most of the weight back on after her wedding and weighed 200 pounds when I learned about the OA meeting.

To be an addict in Hollywood is not an unusual thing, and I thought if I were either an alcoholic or drug addict, that would be quite acceptable! People in show business make lucrative deals at AA Meetings. I, on the other hand, was addicted to sugar in all forms: ice cream, cake, pie, and anything sweet. My favorite was honey-drenched, pull-apart cake. The night before I went to my first twelve-step meeting, I sliced a piece of the honey-crusted cake and wrapped the rest up, but before I knew it, I had unwrapped, resliced, re-wrapped, and eaten half of that cake.

I finally went to a twelve-step program for food. I didn't make any business deals there, but I did learn how to eat to lose weight and how sugar was affecting my temperament, which still took quite a while to change.

At my first meeting, I heard "my" stories from the other participants and realized there was finally a label I could put on what I was doing: I was a compulsive overeater and I was addicted too sugar. It took six months to get the weight off. Actually, I got a little too thin, so I put some back on, and I've maintained it for over twenty years. I did exactly what I was told with the food plan, which is all weighed and measured. I still eat that way to this day, over twenty years later.

Chapter Seventeen

I went to Paris twice in 1990, and by that time I knew how to save money by using a local crew, although by now my husband also traveled and worked with me. Having my husband at my side made this part of my career the best yet. Everything from this time on was a team effort.

The first trip to Paris was to do interviews for the film *Mister Frost*, starring Jeff Goldblum, Kathy Baker and Alan Bates. I had always loved Alan and was thrilled to finally meet him. He was very charming and we flirted with each other during our

interview. I was surprised to read on the Internet after his death in 2003 that he was bisexual. He was married for over twenty years to Victoria Ward and fathered two sons. After his wife's death in 1992, Alan always had women companions, but it was reported that he didn't even admit to them that he had gay lovers.

Reba Merrill

I went back to Paris for the film *Impromptu*, starring Mandy Patinkin, Bernadette Peters, Emma Thompson and Hugh Grant. I was very excited because we were working on location outside of the city in a beautiful château. The film was about the famous nineteenth-century woman writer who used the *nom de plume* George Sand (played by Judy Davis) and fell in love with the composer Frederic Chopin (played by Hugh Grant).

We shot Grant playing the piano for the behind-the-scenes footage, and I asked him, "Did you take piano lessons?"

He said, "No, absolutely not!"

I didn't pick up that he was joking, and I thought he was telling the truth.

When I interviewed Grant again in 1995 for the film *Nine Months* for 20th Century Fox International, I said, "I was surprised to learn you really knew how to play the piano."

It wasn't a question; I was just making a statement that I didn't understand his humor. I was about to learn another lesson because he managed to "blackball" me from every film he did after that because he didn't like that I called him on his behavior.

Sometimes, I am surprised I worked at all, but the films kept coming in.

Going on location was always an adventure. I didn't know until I got there what kind of accommodations I would get. When Judi Schwam hired me once again, she joined me on the trip to a small island in Fiji for the film *Return to the Blue Lagoon*. To get there, we had to fly in three different planes that kept getting smaller. On the last flight, before boarding, we had to be weighed along with our luggage—a humiliating experience for me since I was always conscious of my weight.

There were not enough hotel rooms available, so we had to stay on a dive boat. My cameraman agreed to work at a reduced rate if he could dive during his time off. A speedboat would take us to the set and bring us dinner in the evening. It was like a slumber party on the boat because in addition to Judi and me, there was also a young woman writer from a national magazine who joined us. It was gorgeous in Fiji and we had a great time shooting there.

By 1990, I had learned to play the Hollywood game. I was working, but my deal with production companies was usually barter or a smaller fee on a low-budget film. Since Hollywood is all about "What have you done lately?" I looked like I was working to the outside world but not really making a profit, only just enough to pay my bills.

During this time, I interviewed Keanu Reeves and Peter Falk in *Tune in Tomorrow* and Michael Caine, who starred in *Shock to the System*. Judging from a story Michael told me, his mother sounded like mine. He said his mother never talked with him about his career but would never let her friends forget who her son was. I know my mother talked about me to her friends, but it wasn't until she was dying that she told me she was proud of me.

I then was asked to go to Russia to work on the film *The Ice Runner*, starring Timothy Bottoms and Pat Morita. Instead of being paid, I was given airfare and accommodations in a hotel not usually frequented by Americans. The room was not up to

Reba Merrill

our standards, with bath towels the size of dishtowels, one water spigot for the sink and the bathtub, and phone wires hanging out of the wall that we got fixed by offering someone Marlboros and Tootsie Rolls. It was really a glimpse into how Russians lived at that time. My father was born in the Ukraine and I saw a lot of people who looked like me when I had dark hair. It was difficult being on my twelve-step program diet since they put salt and sugar in everything, so my husband had to taste it first. I think I ate horsemeat, but I made sure it was in a four-ounce portion!

The cast was freezing and the crew had technical problems that resulted in the film never getting finished. *The Ice Runner* was re-cast and re-shot and released in 1992 starring Edward Albert, since the original stars turned down the offer to go back and finish the film.

Chapter Eighteen

When I returned from Russia, there was a message on my answering machine from Teri Ritzer, who (as I mentioned in Chapter 5) had become vice president of international publicity at 20th Century Fox. Previously, I had worked with Teri at Universal on many films starting with Mask and we always had a good relationship.

The message was, "I have behind-the-scenes footage from *For the Boys* and interviews you can't re-shoot, and I need you to re-edit and save it because this stuff is terrible, and I don't know what I can pay you."

Welcome to the world of international publicity! Little did I know that that message was going to change my life. What was interesting about this was that I had already closed my office because I wasn't bringing in enough money, and I had no place to work. I quickly bought a townhouse in Santa Monica and set it up as a full office. We had an edit bay and a conference room, which was really the living room/dining room, and we had a loft that was my assistant's office. It was beautiful, and with Cheryl's help we got all new equipment.

Once we started working on press junkets, we weren't allowed to take photos with the celebrities or ask for autographs at the interviews.

Our first job at the beginning of 1991 was *For the Boys*, starring Bette Midler and James Caan. I discovered when I went through all the footage, which someone else had shot, that there were some amazing sound bites with Bette Midler that nobody had ever thought to use. I looked at the interviews differently and wanted to know what made a performer like Bette excited and scared, and what drove her. I cut this piece differently than they had for the profile for domestic release, which had shown the brassy Bette. When I cut it for international distribution, I showed a softer side of Bette through the scenes that I picked from the movie. This profile was produced only for the international marketplace and had a different rhythm than for an American audience. It was a different pace, so that you could get into what made these people tick.

That was the beginning of the most exciting career I could've ever imagined. The new me, sixty pounds thinner and committed to the twelve-step program, was hired to do celebrity profiles on films for international distribution shown in over sixty countries as well as half-hour specials. Now I was enjoying the process and was really surprised because a different woman was emerging. My binge eating was gone, and I was more aware of my anger and rage and tried control it.

Before I started working again in '91, I went to the spa at Canyon Ranch and registered for the lecture series. It was all about what was important to you to live a better life. In one of the programs we were asked, "If you're on a sinking ship and you can only take one thing or person with you to be saved, who or what would you take?"

I answered without hesitation "my career." I probably never should have told my family what I said, but in all honesty, I was totally identified by my career and it was the most important thing in my life. I think that is probably true for a lot of men, but most people think women should put their families first.

I started working for a third studio, Sony Pictures Entertainment, Inc. in addition to Fox and Buena Vista. It was amazing how it happened. I didn't know Adam Gordon, who phoned me and said, "I called the duplicating house that does most of our electronic press kits and asked who was the best EPK producer. Your name came up, so I want you to do a budget and a proposal for an international half-hour show on *The Indian in the Cupboard*."

I went to an afternoon matinee of the film, and it was just a bunch of kids and me. It was a kid's movie but really quite interesting, so I came up with the idea that great children's books make marvelous movies.

I called Marvin Levy, who worked for Steven Spielberg, and explained, "I'm going to do a half-hour show on Melissa Mathison and how she has turned good children's stories into even greater films." The screenplay for *The Indian in the*

Cupboard was written by Melissa Mathison, who also wrote *E.T, the Extra-Terrestrial*. Steven Spielberg worked with Melissa to develop the story for *E. T.*, which was based on an imaginary friend he had as a child. I asked if I could get permission from Steven to use a clip from *E.T.*

Marvin called me back and said, "Steven loves Melissa, and we will pull a clip for you." They had never done that before, so I asked him to send me a fax (in 1995 I wasn't using e-mail yet) to confirm they were sending a clip for my special on *The Indian in the Cupboard*.

Then I called MGM, told them that I was doing a special on great children's films, and asked for a clip from *The Wizard of Oz*, adding that I had a clip from *E.T.* Like magic, the door opened, the clips I wanted to use came in, and I wrote and submitted the proposal for my special. Although there was another company bidding on the project, I was hired.

When my competition asked "Why?" He was told it was because I had a clip from *E.T.* Since he knew Spielberg hadn't ever released clips from the film, his shocked response was, "That's not fair!"

Melissa was married to Harrison Ford at that time. He flew her down to Los Angeles with their kids in their own plane from Wyoming just to do the interview.

The Indian in the Cupboard special, called "Lights, Camera, Magic," led to twenty-three more documentary specials for Sony Pictures, ranging from action heroes to romantic films to thrillers. We had a great time working on them. You can see the complete list of the specials at: http://www.imdb.com/company/co0095329.

Chapter Nineteen

The international market place opened the door to interviews over the next fifteen years with some of the most famous stars in the world. I interviewed Robin Williams many times, a man so fast and funny that I had to be sure to do two things before sitting down with him I had to know where I wanted to go with the interview. I also had to be sure, as I had learned with Dustin Hoffman, to go to the bathroom because when someone makes me laugh that hard, it could be embarrassing.

During my first interview with Robin for *Toys*, I made a really big mistake that almost ruined our audio track. For his role in *Toys*, he wore an outrageous jacket that made all kinds of sounds and beats. He brought it to the junket, and I thought it would be clever to have him wear the funny jacket. He played those sounds during the interview, and it made me laugh, which could be heard on our soundtrack.

I asked him if he thought people were born funny. He joked, "If you get dropped. That's what happened to me. I was in a drug store, and this lovely lady named Susie was taking care of me, and I fell off the chair and I think everything changed from that moment."

I interviewed Robin again the next year for *Mrs. Doubtfire* for use in a half-hour show I produced for Fox. To prepare him to play the role of a woman, they had to wax him all over because he is so hairy, a very painful process. He was a good sport since he knew this film was good for his career, and he was a perfect fit to play *Mrs. Doubtfire*. I sat down with him for nearly forty minutes, and he was a charmer—even though he tried to destroy me with laughter. Most comics are great dramatic actors, and he is no exception.

Once again, thanks to Teri Ritzer Meyer, who by now had added her married name and become a senior vice president at Buena Vista International (a division of Disney), I interviewed Robin Williams, this time for *Jack*. The film starred Robin as a ten-year-old boy who is growing so fast that he looks like a forty-year-old man. I was excited about working on *Jack* because the director was Francis Ford Coppola. Even though by this point, I had interviewed many celebrities and directors, it was one of the thrills of my life to talk to the legendary Academy Award-winning director of *Godfather I, II* and *III*, as well as other classic films like *Patton* and *Apocalypse Now*.

I discovered while doing the research for my questions that Coppola had polio as a child and had spent a lot of time in bed making puppets and telling stories; as a director, he got to live his childhood dreams. It was a wonderful opportunity to sit down with a man who was so talented, but who had also faced hard times.

The critics panned Jack and wrote that Coppola was too talented to be making this type of film. Coppola defended it, saying that he was not ashamed of it and had always wanted to work with Robin Williams, who was a friend of his. Williams only agreed to star in Jack when Coppola signed on as director.

Robin's big break came in the form of a space alien on the TV series *Mork & Mindy* in the seventies. I asked him if it had been difficult to tell his father, who was a big auto company executive, that he was going to go into show business.

"He said, 'If you really love it, I'll support you in that.' Which is great. 'But I want you to have an alternate profession just in case you can't find work'. He recommended welding or animal proctology!"

In 1993, I was invited to interview Sean Connery for the film *Rising Sun*. I was excited until I got there and was attacked by a fat, mean publicist who blacklisted me after hearing a lie that I was selling my interviews to TV stations. She greeted me with, "Why are you here? We don't need you, and don't ask him about James Bond." Of course, the role of Bond was what Connery was most remembered for, so that put me on edge; I wanted to make sure I wouldn't slip and get into more trouble with her.

I asked Sean about his time on *The Man Who Would Be King*, a film he had starred in with Michael Caine in 1975, which was shot in Morocco, even though the story was set in India. When they went to a club, they weren't allowed to bring their

Nearly Famous

wives. I wanted to know if it was true that he wanted to dance with Michael's driver because he was better looking. He said, laughing, "That is absolutely true."

He then told me about a frightening incident that had happened there. He liked to drive himself to and from the set; it was very hot, so he took off his turban but left his caftan and makeup on. He told me, "Something went wrong somewhere and there were riots. I was driving back and I drove straight into the guys firing the guns. I didn't speak their language. And these guys were seriously dragging me out of the car. And, just by luck, one of them recognized me as James Bond. Otherwise I would have still been there."

With that line, he opened the door to talk about Bond, so I said, "you have had this amazing career outside of your role as Bond."

He replied, "Why have you been avoiding Bond?"

I said that I was told not to ask about that role. "What do you think I would do?"

"Kiss me but I don't think that is the way it works." He laughed and I was finally able to breathe.

He was quite charming and still handsome without hair, which I didn't even notice was gone. I have to admit my heart did flutter when he said his famous line, "Bond, James Bond."

I like doing research, so I am always prepared with some questions about the star's background, not just the film they are promoting. Harrison Ford appreciates people who are respectful of him and his time by doing their homework.

I told him, "Don't worry about the questions. I know all the answers." Saying that made the difference in getting a great interview with him. One of the stories he told me was about when he was shooting a film in Morocco. He and his wife at the time, Melissa Mathison, drove to a small village with one movie theater with two screens, and both of them were playing his movies.

His wife turned to him and said, "I guess you're famous." I was amazed that he was willing to be so open and tell me that story, since he is really very shy and uncomfortable talking about himself.

He also told me, "It is very useful to me in selling movies to be well known. The problem that I have is that the most valuable thing you have to give up in your life is anonymity – to be able to pass unnoticed through life when you want to. I have learned over a period of time as I become more and more in public view to deal with the reality of that situation. There are practical means to stay as small as you can in public and not attract attention to yourself."

When I interviewed Harrison for *Air Force One*, the first question I asked him was, "You play some of the best heroes in films. Are you getting back at the bullies who used to beat you up at school?" He was surprised I knew about that, since he said he only told one person, and they had the nerve to put it on the Internet.

"What happened was that I moved to a new school and there was already a well-formed society, and because I was the outsider, I didn't fit in. The school sport became throwing me off the edge of the parking lot down a twenty-foot bank every recess…My reaction was just to pick myself up, dust myself off, and crawl up to the top again. I developed great sympathy from the girls, so while I was getting thrown off the hill at recess, I was gaining a benefit that lasted through the rest of the day."

Harrison didn't start out intending to be an actor and thought about doing voiceovers. "I had taken a course in drama without realizing that it involved a stage appearance. It was nerve wracking. My first ambition was to overcome that fear. Then I became involved, after that fear dissipated, in the other processes that made acting interesting to me. The interest in story- telling and the effect that was created between myself and the audience—they helped me find a place in society that I hadn't felt before."

He didn't get a job in voice-overs, but he was cast in guest roles on various TV shows. "What I was anxious to do was play with the big boys. I wanted to do ambitious kinds of films and take on characters that were a bit more complicated and interesting. And I was aware that if I stayed at the same place doing episodic television over and over again, I would wear out my face and never get a chance to do the kind of work I wanted to do. And because I discovered another way of putting food on the table for my young family by doing carpentry, I was able to wait it out."

There are still homes in West L.A. with cabinets with Ford's signature. George Lucas discovered him when he was hired to build cabinets in his home. "I always knew that tenacity was more important than anything else. I arrived in Hollywood with a metaphoric bus of young people who all had a similar ambition as mine, and as the years went by, the attrition rate eliminated many of those people from the competition pool. Finally there were only a few of us left from that 'entering class.' I always saw life that way: that you really had to stick it out to prevail. And, of course, along the way I learned a great deal more about my craft than I knew when I first started."

George Lucas asked Harrison to read lines with the other actors when he was auditioning for *Star Wars*. Lucas eventually cast him for his breakout role as Han Solo. "I was thirty-five when I first did *Star Wars*, so I was even older than that when I did Indiana Jones." That iconic character became his signature role in a series of films beginning with *Raiders of the Lost Ark*. As a result of those blockbuster movies and all their sequels, he currently is the third-highest grossing US box-office star.

"The job is always the same," he told me. "It's to help tell the story through character behavior. Certainly there are some experiences that are more fun to go through than others. Sometimes filmmaking is very difficult, very complex, and other times it is a ball to go to work every day. I love making movies. I love the opportunity to live different lives, to work with different people on different kinds of subjects. I love getting to travel and play with the big toys that are involved in movie making. I have, I think, the best job in the world."

When I am interviewing someone, I am always aware that studio execs are watching me from a control room, and I concentrate so intently that I don't hear anything except the answers to my questions. During one of our interviews, Harrison looked at me and said, "The tape stopped and we're not finished yet. Put another tape in." I was scheduled for a twenty-minute interview with him, and they had put in a ten-minute tape by mistake, but he was willing to keep going for the next ten minutes.

The publicist at the studio told me later that he wasn't always charming and cooperative with other interviewers, but he knew that I cared enough to do the research and he respected me for that. One time when he greeted me with, "So good to see you again," I was so surprised I actually turned around to see who he was talking to!

As I mentioned earlier in the book, the first time I interviewed Harrison was when I was still working on my talk show in San Diego and he was promoting Star *Wars*. I had forgotten about it until years later, when I found some film reels in a brown-paper grocery bag in the storage room. I asked my son-in-law, Richard, who is a successful editor, to transfer it to videotape to see what was on it and he told me, "You have an interview with Harrison Ford."

I was surprised to see that one of the things I said to him in the interview was, "Boy, are your eyes beautiful!" Today, I would rather cut my tongue out than say anything like that again in an interview!

Chapter Twenty

I expect to see powerful performances when two Oscar winners star in a film, and I am never disappointed.

I interviewed Al Pacino for the spy thriller *The Recruit* in 2003. By that point in his career, he had appeared in over thirty films, most with critical acclaim, had received dozens of award nominations, and had won an Oscar for Best Actor for Scent of a Woman.

Like many of the stars I interviewed, he told me that he was drawn to performing at an early age. "When I was very little, movies were my only connection to the world, really. My mother worked, and when she came home she would take me to the picture show…I was so enamored with the film that when I came home, I would want to relive the film again and so I would play all the roles I saw. I had this ability to mimic. I would mimic the movies. I would mimic any of the current singers, whether it was Al Jolson or Sinatra or whoever it was. Then I learned how to mimic situations and people just for the fun of it."

Al grew up in the South Bronx. He acted in school plays and then in New York's theatrical underground, but was rejected for the Actors Studio when he was still a teenager.

"I think what happens is that you learn to forgive yourself. You see in the scheme of things how it is, and you say, 'Well, I tried.' The worst thing, as they say, is not to go for it. But if you go for it, it is out of your hands, like that old saying: 'What anyone says about me is none of my business.' You hope for the best and you see that a lot of the times, things happen and you have no control over them."

He was finally accepted into the Actors Studio when he was twenty-six and now serves as co-president with Ellen Burstyn and Harvey Keitel. Starting with his breakout role as Michael Corleone in *The Godfather* in 1972, he is recognized as one of the greatest actors in film history and was given the Lifetime Achievement Award in 2007 by the American Film Institute.

"Sometimes I am a little bit blinded by the attention, so I don't make correct assessments. I was fortunate to have certain things happen in my life. Persisting in something – he who persists in his folly will one day be wise. I haven't gotten wise yet, but I keep persisting."

Persistence is another quality I can relate to and had in common with Al Pacino, as well as many of the stars I interviewed. Persistence is what kept me going when I couldn't find a job at the start of my TV career and, despite seventeen rejections, I didn't give up after being fired from my last on-camera job. I persisted until I created a new career for myself, off-camera, doing celebrity profiles—the work I loved most of all.

I interviewed Denzel Washington five times over the years. When I sat down with him for *Remember the Titans* in 2000, I gave him a video for his children of the educational program based on the film *Glory* that I was asked to produce for Eastman Kodak. It was distributed to one hundred thousand schools to teach children about the African-American soldiers fighting in the Civil War, the subject of the movie that earned Denzel his first Oscar.

When Denzel Washington was a young boy, the local fortuneteller told his mother that someday he would entertain millions. He told me, "That woman prophesized that I would speak to millions of people—and I guess she was right."

After graduating from high school, Denzel enrolled at Fordham University to study journalism. "I never knew about acting. I never knew anyone who was in acting. I had no desire to be one. There wasn't anybody on the air that looked like me that made me want to be one."

That all changed after he took his first acting class. "They just happened to be having auditions and I got the lead role in a play the first time I read for one." After graduation, he moved to San Francisco, enrolled at the American Conservatory Theater, and left after only one year to find work as an actor.

"I remember the first film I ever did—it was *Carbon Copy*—and I said to myself, 'This is just a natural world for me. This feels comfortable.' I was naïve about it. I found out shortly thereafter when I did my stint of 'no work' that you do what you've got to do until you can do what you want to do. I remember after *Carbon Copy* being in the unemployment office and seeing someone I knew in line C, and they were like, 'What are you doing in here, man? I just saw you starring in a movie.' I said, 'I'm getting my $126, or whatever it was, and fifty cents and I am waiting to get to line B just like you are.' A humbling experience."

Denzel kept auditioning for parts and won the lead role to play civil rights activist *Malcolm X* in an off-Broadway production of *When the Chickens Come Home to Roost*, a role that he would later play again in the film *Malcolm X*.

"People were coming down to see me. I mean, I met everybody doing this little play for $125 a week. Diana Ross would be there one night and Muhammad Ali would be there the next night. It felt like I was beginning to arrive in the New York theater community... I remember looking out at the audience and thinking, I really like this. I already knew that was going to be my lifelong profession and I had found my quote, unquote, calling."

His big break came the next year when he was cast as Dr. Phillip Chandler in the TV series *St Elsewhere*. In 1987 his movie career took off with his role as South African activist Steve Biko in *Cry Freedom*, which earned him his first Oscar and several Golden Globe nominations. Denzel is the only African-American actor to receive two Academy Awards.

"I didn't get into this business to become a famous movie star. It was more about the work. It is still more about the work, but the whole machine is accelerating. You see, if you have a little talent, it grinds you up before you really have a chance to develop your talent. I was fortunate to get a chance to develop."

He has been married to his wife, Pauletta, since 1983. "I'm a father first. I don't get life mixed up with making a living. I was there for all four of my children being born. When the first one was born, I recognized the difference between life and making a living... Acting is making a living. The one thing I am most happy about in terms of my career is the fact that I got there by the grace of God first of all, but short of that, I got there just by working hard. Not partying with the right people, not compromising myself in any way or cutting any kind of deals—just by working hard and by plugging along, 'sawing wood' as I like to call it. I am a twenty-year overnight sensation."

While writing about Denzel, I realized that I also felt like a twenty-year overnight sensation, still successful in my career at an age when most people were starting to retire. There are advantages to being able to work as you get older. It's what made me want to get up in the morning. I was motivated, stimulated, and excited about the work I was doing, like so many of the stars I interviewed.

Chapter Twenty-one

After interviewing so many male stars, it was refreshing to talk to some leading ladies who revealed much more about themselves to me than their male counterparts.

I interviewed Angelina Jolie several times over the years. The first time was for *The Bone Collector* when she was twenty-four. It was 1999, and even though I had been off sugar for ten years, the one thing I remember most about the interview is seeing the Gummy Bears that her makeup artist carried in her Lucite bag. It was apparently a treat for Angie while she was working on a film. Maybe she liked sugar as much as I did.

Known as one of the most beautiful women in the world, I asked her if her looks got in the way. She told me, "Honestly, I don't feel very confident about myself. I have a lot of insecurities. I wear black all the time, and people think it's because it is so cool and mysterious, but it's really because I'm a big slob and spill stuff."

Angelina is one of the few actresses also known as an action hero for her roles as Lara Croft and Evelyn Salt in films where she does a lot of her own stunts. "I have worked with the same stunt team for ten years and they have become my family. And if they say, 'you can go off that bridge,' I'll trust them that it is okay."

She has an on-again, off-again relationship with her father, actor Jon Voigt. When he played the role of her father in *Lara Croft: Tomb Raider* in 2001, one of the scenes poignantly mirrored what may have been going on between them when they say to each other, "I missed you."

When I asked Angie if anything scared her, she replied, "Feeling that I am incapable of doing something scares me. I am only afraid of something happening to the people I love. That's the great fear for everybody."

Just like so many of the stars I interviewed, she told me, "I think you can do anything you set your mind to." I agree.

Angie starred with Brad Pitt in *Mr. & Mrs. Smith*, and they started a relationship that led to his divorce from Jennifer

Aniston. I interviewed Jennifer for five different films and when I sat down with her for *Derailed*, rumors were all over the tabloids that Angelina was pregnant with Brad's baby. I felt sorry for Jennifer because the breakup was so public.

The theme of *Derailed* was infidelity and its consequences. I told the studio executive that I was going to ask Jennifer a question about infidelity, and they said that she would never answer it.

Surprisingly, she did: "I think it will absolutely make people think twice about infidelity, because you never know. It's Russian roulette, isn't it? You never know when one is going to blow up in your face."

Angie and Brad currently have three biological children and three adopted children from various parts of the world. Brad and Angie are known for their humanitarian work, and she is a Goodwill Ambassador for the United Nations.

I interviewed Brad Pitt for the film Seven ten years before he and Angie became a couple, and met a much different man than he appears to be today. It was difficult to edit his profile then because he didn't finish his thoughts or sentences. When I see him interviewed today on TV, he appears more confident and more committed, not only to Angie and their family but also to making a contribution to the world. What a difference a decade can make in someone's life.

I interviewed Julia Roberts for *Runaway Bride* in 1999. By that time, she had been in a string of successful films. In *Runaway Bride*, she was teamed again with her leading man Richard Gere and director Garry Marshall, who cast her in *Pretty Woman*.

When I asked her if she performed around the house growing up, she replied, "I come from a family of performers. I guess in an unconscious way, we were always entertaining one another, but I didn't put on plays or shows. I did have the occasional flea-market dress-up moment. I had this one Spanish yellow gown that I would wear and play my ukulele for my dad. I guess that was performing."

I asked her if she was living out her dreams and if she ever asked herself, "Why me?" She said, "I guess it is about gratitude.

Nearly Famous

Sometimes I do become so overwhelmed with an appreciation and gratitude for the blessings of my life that you do have to say, I don't know if it is 'Why me?' but 'I don't know why it's me, but I'm going with it.'"

Like Angelina, Julia is known as one of the most beautiful and famous women in the world. I wanted to know how she dealt with fame.

Julia responded, "I think the perception of what it's like to be me or just to be famous is a lot more daunting than the reality of it. I am a person who is famous, but I am also a sister and good at a dinner party, and I am also a lot of things. It is just another tag on a long list of stuff."

Since that interview she has added wife to Danny Moder and mother to Hazel, Finn and Henry, along with Academy Award-winning actress to her list of accomplishments. "I think everything is a choice, and you can choose to go through it effortlessly or you can choose to have it be a struggle."

By the time I interviewed Julia Roberts, I was making better choices in my life. I had been in a twelve-step program for almost ten years and my life was no longer a struggle. I didn't see it then, but I realized while writing this book how often the things a star said in an interview paralleled my own life. I was living my dreams then and realize now that I was asking questions of the stars I wished someone had asked me.

The studio executives were watching me from a control room, so I had to be careful about what I said during the interview. After the mikes were turned off, I told Julia that I had not been allowed to interview her before because her former publicist was on a power trip and would not let me work with any of her clients.

Julia was surprised to discover that something so unprofessional was being done in her name. Hollywood is a small town and word gets around, so I found out later that I wasn't the only one who was treated badly. The publicist was mean to everyone except her clients, who eventually fired her.

Chapter Twenty-two

Beauty and talent don't always lead to a happy ending in Hollywood, as sadly is shown here with the two extraordinary women I interviewed.

As I am writing this, the tabloids are focused on the 911 call about Demi Moore's reported collapse and seizure from "smoking something" and the problems in her career and marriage. Everyone knows that she is forty-nine; although she was the first actress to pass the $10 million salary mark, she is now facing ageism in Hollywood and reportedly not handling it well. She has mostly played the beautiful leading lady and femme fatale, roles usually not offered to someone almost fifty. I know what that feels like, since I was burned by ageism when a woman half my age replaced me on my talk show when I was only forty-four.

I interviewed Demi for *G. I. Jane* (1997). When I saw her shave her head in the film, it reminded me of my mother. More specifically, it made me realize how vulnerable she must have felt when she lost her hair from chemotherapy and didn't want me to see her that way. I talked about my mother's feelings about being bald – which I don't think another journalist would have done at a press junket – and asked Demi how she coped with actually being bald.

She told me, "To do this, you have to step inside for all to see a depth of vulnerability that most of us don't want anybody to see, which is where you pull your strength from … Most people view vulnerability as exposing something that shows weakness, and in fact, it is the exact opposite, and I think that is why we are so attracted to it in other people."

Was she surprised where she ended up? "No, because I had a blind faith, and I have no idea where it came from or why. And I don't know why I thought I should be doing it. There was just that other thing that said, 'you need to go do this and it's okay'… It was gut and instinct and intuition. My career is different and more wonderful and more horrible [laughs] than I imagined. I do know the sort of person I am, and that is what's most important. You have to just go in blindly. Just go full force with complete commitment, focus, and do it. It is not that I don't have fear. It is just what I do with it. That would make the difference."

If someone asked me if I was surprised at where I ended up, I would have to say, "yes and no." My parents raised me to be a wife and mother, so I didn't know if I would ever have a career. After I divorced my first husband, I married a man who believed in me, told me I was beautiful and that I could do anything. Just like Demi, I went into my career full-force with complete commitment and focus, and just did it.

When I interviewed Whitney Houston for the remake of *The Preacher's Wife* with Denzel Washington, I asked her how success had changed her. She told me, "Success doesn't change you—fame does. You've got a whole world of people calling your name and you really don't know them."

As I was completing this book, that "world of people" was mourning the loss of "the Leading Lady of Pop." Her sudden death on February 11, 2012 at the age of forty-eight, ironically the night before the Grammys, stunned the music community that paid tribute to her at the awards ceremony. Whitney was a multiple Grammy winner and one of the best-selling female recording artists in the world.

Whitney was thirty-two when we sat down together, four years after she made her film debut in *The Bodyguard* starring with Kevin Costner. I said to her, "I think you live a life that is like a fairytale, but I bet you have down days just like everybody. How do you deal with them?"

She answered, "There is a misconception that when we become famous, we live these beautiful, perfect lives and that nothing is ever on a low. It's a bad conception because then people think you have to be this grand old person who is just happy about life and everything because we've got money. Money doesn't make you happy. It never did. History will tell you that. And fame certainly doesn't make you happy. People will tell you that who are famous."

Nearly Famous

After her 1992 marriage to singer Bobby Brown, Whitney descended into a very public battle with substance abuse, which could have led to her untimely death. I can relate to Whitney's struggle, since I know that I am one bite away from being out of control again, and it scares me because I don't want to go back to that kind of life; once an addict, always an addict.

When her casket was being carried out of the church, her voice could be heard singing "I Will Always Love You," the best-selling single by a female artist in music history.

Chapter Twenty-three

Being able to combine action and comedy is rare in Hollywood, but two actors I enjoyed interviewing not only did it well, but also were so successful that they made a lot of money for themselves as well as the studios.

Before Will Smith became one of the most powerful actors in Hollywood, he was a rapper known as The Fresh Prince. He told me, "At eighteen years old, I had more money and time on my hands than I knew what to do with. I had my ups and downs, and I had money and I lost money."

When Will was in his teens, he teamed up with Jeffrey A. Townes and began performing with him as "DJ Jazzy Jeff and the Fresh Prince"; they won the first Grammy in the Rap category in 1988.

"When I was growing up and started rapping, there were ten guys in my neighborhood who could rap better than me. But none of them went for it. None of them had the drive or the energy to actually pursue it, and I did."

Will was a millionaire before he was twenty and then near bankruptcy when he signed with NBC to star in his own sitcom *The Fresh Prince of Bel Air* when he was twenty-two. "I had all those experiences in the music business, so I was able to come into this level of success with the knowledge of 'self' that would really keep you grounded. And it takes a period of adjusting. My family wasn't rich, so having a few dollars was a little fun. Being presented with another opportunity with television and then into the film world, I just feel I had the greatest education and preparation that you could possibly have."

I interviewed Will for the first time when he starred in *Independence Day*, which was the second-highest grossing film in history at the time in 1996 and established Will's film career. To date, his films have grossed $5.7 billion in global box office. He is the only actor to have eight consecutive films gross over $100 million in the domestic box office.

Will told me, "You want to be a super-hero, and you want to be the guy that saves the world and you get to beat up the bad guys and save the damsel in distress…It feels great to actually get the opportunity to experience it—that inner child comes out. What I have always felt is that you have to focus on whatever you want. Even if you're not sure that this is what you want to do forever, focus on it for now and do it to the best of your ability. I've always been very confident because I've known that the only thing that separates me from anyone else is not talent, not any level of skill; it's just that I do it. There is a part of me that believes there isn't anything I can't do."

That comment really resonated with me because it was the way I approached my career. I focused on what I wanted to do and found a way to make the star-video profiles unique and interesting, which is what the execs at the studios and the TV stations said set me apart from the other entertainment journalists. I just did it and believed there wasn't anything I couldn't do.

I went to my first interview with Johnny Depp in 2003 thinking he was a "bad boy" who liked to tear up hotel suites, which he was charged with doing early in his career in 1994. I was very curious to find out who he really was and if he would share that part of himself with me. I was astounded by how much I liked him, and that the first thing he told me was that he wanted to be a musician, not an actor.

"It's very difficult for me to say that I am an actor because music was and is everything to me. I started playing the guitar early in my twelfth year and became obsessed and basically locked myself in a room for a good year to teach myself and listen to records and pick stuff up…and taught myself how to play. At that moment, that was my world, that was my life… nothing else mattered."

Johnny dropped out of high school and started playing in garage bands and then met Nicholas Cage, who took him to his agent and asked him to get Johnny a small role. "I can remember calling my family, calling my Mom and saying, 'Hey, I got a job.' And she said, 'Oh yeah, what's that?' And I said, 'I guess I am going to do a movie.' And I heard on the other line, 'What kind of movie?'" he said in kind of a gruff tone.

"'No, no, Mom, it's not that. It's kind of a horror film, *Nightmare on Elm Street*, and they are going to pay me 'this much,' and I had never seen that much money in my life... I thought, well, I'll do this movie, and then I will go back to the band and continue playing. I thought it was a one-off, I never thought I would end up acting."

He has been quoted saying that he was paid $1,200 a week for pretty much doing nothing most of the day on that film, pretending to be someone else. "Fame is a word I could never use next to my name...I never understood the fascination with the personal life of a guy who tells lies for a living."

He has come a long way since that first paycheck. He was paid $55 million for *Pirates of the Caribbean: On Stranger Tides*, which was released in 2011. His likeness is the permanent image for Jack Sparrow on the Pirates of the Caribbean rides at Disneyland and Disney World.

"My kids' reaction to the Pirates of the Caribbean ride, the 'papa section' as it is called, was amazing. They were so cute about it. They were jumping up and down. I know they are going to take their kids someday to see Daddy on the ride, their kids are going to take their kids, and I'll still be there. That is just amazing to me."

One of the things I really liked about him was that once he had children, fatherhood became the most important thing in his life. When he was making *Sweeney Todd*—by the way, that's really him singing in the film—his daughter Lily Rose got sick, and he took ten days off from a multi-million dollar production so he could be at her bedside in London. He didn't return to the film until she was out of danger. He recently donated $1 million pounds to the Great Ormand Street Hospital where his daughter was hospitalized in London.

Johnny has had a very successful career for someone who never set out to be an actor. I asked him if he ever asked himself, "Why me?"

He answered, "All the time. It probably happens two to three times a week that I will be in situations when I wonder to myself,

'How did this all happen? How did I get here?' At the same time it is such a great gift, such a blessing. Who am I to ask? I've just got to be thankful. Respect it and keep moving forward."

Ever since that first interview with Johnny, I had wondered why the tone of his voice had briefly changed to gruff when he was recounting to me the conversation with his mom after he got his first film role in *Nightmare on Elm Street*. It wasn't until he did *Public Enemies* in 2009 that I realized he was also likely speaking to his stepfather Robert Palmer. Johnny has described his stepfather, who passed away in 2000, as an inspiration, especially in playing the role of Dillinger in *Public Enemies*. His stepfather served time for robbery in Stateville prison in Joliet, Illinois, where Depp would later shoot scenes for *Public Enemies* and would be shown a mug shot of his stepdad when he was an inmate there.

My second interview with Johnny Depp in 2006 was the last time I ever worked for Disney. At the time, I didn't know I would be moving forward to another phase of my career. Teri Ritzer Meyer, the studio executive who kept hiring me for film after film, told me not to ask Johnny any more questions, but with all the noise in the room I thought she had said, 'Ask more questions.'

Although Johnny didn't seem to mind, Teri never gave me another film after that interview. I found out I was not hired again not just because I made a mistake, but because the way they did international publicity was changing and more of the work was being done in-house. I went out with a bang and couldn't have asked for a better last interview. Johnny Depp never disappointed me and I hope I never disappointed him.

Chapter Twenty-four

From the time I came to Hollywood, I wanted to fit in and vowed to never tell the truth about my age, my weight, or the color of my hair. When I started doing video profiles, TV stations that ran the interviews with my voice wanted to meet me. I didn't want them to find out my age (which you couldn't tell from my voice), so I said to my daughter Cheryl, "You go to meet them so they don't see that I am an old lady."

I was afraid of what would happen if they found out that I was over fifty. I was obsessed with what age had done to my career in the past, since I had gotten fired as TV host and replaced by a much younger woman. I created a fictional backstory that I married a man with two daughters whose wife had died, and I had adopted them. I called Cheryl my daughter but didn't want people to think I had given birth to her and figure out my age. I didn't know at the time that Cheryl, who worked with me and was my editor for twenty years, was upset that I never gave her a "heads-up" before she found out from someone else that I was telling people this lie.

She just told me recently that someone came up to her at a party and said, "Reba is such a wonderful woman to raise you as her own daughter," which left Cheryl hurt and speechless. With so much nepotism in Hollywood, when I introduced her as my editor instead of my daughter, I thought it was a compliment since it looked like I hired her because of her talent, not as a favor. She didn't see it that way, which led to some hard feelings, which we have now resolved.

I had a big black-tie dinner dance for my fiftieth birthday and told everybody that it was my fortieth. And when I turned sixty, I said I was fifty. When I turned seventy, I couldn't say that number or grasp the concept of being that age. I didn't want to celebrate with a birthday party and had a housewarming instead. Only my family knew it was my birthday.

When I turned seventy-five, I had stopped working on films, so I came out and finally admitted how old I really was. But

Reba Merrill

no one believed me because of the Evite I sent for my birthday party, which stated: "For decades, European women have been adding years to their age so people would tell them how good they looked. Please join Reba for her '75th' for dinner and conversation." For the first time, I had said my age in public, and still people said they didn't believe me.

Epilogue

The program has worked for me since December 17, 1989, when I was taken to my first OA meeting. I have never left and still attend three meetings a week. I know that I am addicted to sugar, which a recent report on *60 Minutes* called as toxic and addicting as cocaine. I take it one day at a time and if I need something sweet, I eat fruit or a treat with a sugar substitute. The extra sixty pounds I gained came off in six months. The emotional baggage took much longer—some of it still lingers. I now know the difference between emotional eating and eating when I am really hungry. That is worth everything to me; I learned that if I change my response to the action that triggers overeating, I stop feeling hungry. I get out of the room where there is food and go for a walk or go to bed, and the hunger passes in ten minutes. That is how I have kept the weight off for over twenty years.

When I lost the weight, I was uncomfortable with compliments, which was surprising to me. The weight owned the room and so nobody noticed how old I was. Now that I have kept the weight off, they say, "Gee, you look good for your age." I was able to bury my fears about aging by carrying all that extra weight. I am sure my behavior was worse than I remembered. There is a lot I didn't remember which only came back while writing this book. I am so grateful for the career I had interviewing celebrities and promoting their films—the people I met, the places I went, and the lifestyle it afforded me. This book gives me a chance to fondly look back. I wouldn't change a thing.

Today, I most appreciate the fact that I did not achieve that level of success until I was in my mid-forties. I was lucky to achieve success much later in life, so I had an understanding of the importance of being at the right place at the right time. The truth is that I made plenty of mistakes. They all led me here, and here is just fine with me.

Acknowledgements

In Hollywood it's who you know and who knows you. All these people gave me a chance, helping me along the way: Tony Angellotti, Marvin Antonowsky, Roger Armstrong, Henri Bollinger, Hilary Clark, Pamela Godfrey, Adam Gordon, Michael Harpster, Jan Kean, Pat Kingsley, Christina Kounelias, Marvin Levy, Arlene Ludwig, Teri Ritzer Meyer, Terry Press, Michele Reese, Linda Brown Salomone, Judi Schwam, Bill Shields, Susan van der Werff, Frank Wright, Fran Zell.

Every book needs a great editor, I found one in Edward Friedel. He worked diligently and didn't pull any punches helping me to make my life come to life.

This book would not have been finished without the help and encouragement of Ginny Weissman. She not only helped me to order my thoughts but also pushed me to dig deeper when writing about my addiction.

My biggest thanks has to be extended to my terrific daughter, Cheryl Hiltzik, who took my interviews and edited them into remarkable stories that played on TV stations all over the world. I owe her my career, as I could not have done it without her.

Thank you to those who took the time to read my book: Pete Hammond, your words touched me. Pat Kingsley, your comments moved me. Stu Samuels, thanks for the pat on the back. Mark DeCarlo, I am grateful for your insights. Winona Phillabaum, my local librarian, I was overwhelmed by your very kind words.

Finally, I want to acknowledge the two women who were instrumental in jump starting and keeping my career going. Dee Wallace, whose compelling interview played a major role in convincing TV stations to use materials which they did not create. She also cared enough to write the foreword for the book. As a woman working in Hollywood, it's not only what you can do, but how you look doing it. Doctor Karyn Grossman, my talented dermatologist, did that for me.

Reba has conducted nearly 1000 interviews. This is a partial list of celebtrities.

Ben Affleck
Tim Allen
Gillian Anderson
Wes Anderson
Julie Andrews
Jennifer Aniston
Tom Arnold
Rosanna Arquette
Hal Ashby
Richard Attenborough
Dan Aykroyd
Christian Bale
Anne Bancroft
Antonio Banderas
Ellen Barkin
Drew Barrymore
Kim Basinger
Alan Bates
Michael Bay
Kate Beckinsale
Monica Bellucci
Maria Bello
Tom Berenger
Cate Blanchett
Orlando Bloom
Benjamin Bratt
Jeff Bridges
Matthew Broderick
Adrian Brody
Albert Brooks
Pierce Brosnan
Jerry Bruckheimer
Sandra Bullock
Ellen Burstyn
Tim Burton
Gabriel Byrne
Nicholas Cage
Michael Caine
Martin Campbell
James Cameron
Kirk Cameron
Lynda Carter
Jim Carrey
Dana Carvey
Jim Caviezel
Jackie Chan
Kyle Chandler
Stockard Channing
Chevy Chase
Cher
Rae Dawn Chong
Glenn Close
James Coburn
Chris Columbus
Sean Connery
Frances Ford Coppola
Billy Crudup
Russell Crowe
Tom Cruise
Jamie Lee Curtis
Joan Cusack
John Cusack
Willem Dafoe
Claire Danes
Blythe Danner
Daniel Day-Lewis
Patrick Dempsey
Judi Dench

Reba Merrill

Johnny Depp
Laura Dern
Leonardo DiCaprio
Vin Diesel
Roger Donaldson
Michael Douglas
Kirk Douglas
Robert Downey, Jr.
Minnie Driver
David Duchovny
Faye Dunaway
Kirsten Dunst
Clint Eastwood
Blake Edwards
Jenna Elfman
Roland Emmerich
Robert Englund
Colin Farrell
Chow Yun-Fat
Sally Field
Albert Finney
Lawrence Fishburne
Mick Fleetwood
Bridget Fonda
Peter Fonda
Harrison Ford
Jodie Foster
Michael J. Fox
Brendan Fraser
Stephen Frears
Antoine Fuqua
Janeane Garofalo
Andy Garcia
James Garner
Richard Gere
Mel Gibson
Danny Glover

Whoopi Goldberg
Jeff Goldblum
Cuba Gooding, Jr.
Ginnifer Goodwin
Hugh Grant
Melanie Griffith
Carla Gugino
Gene Hackman
Tom Hanks
Renny Harlin
Robert Harling
Josh Hartnett
Anne Hathaway
Goldie Hawn
Anne Heche
Dustin Hoffman
Anthony Hopkins
Bob Hoskins
Whitney Houston
Bryce Dallas Howard
Ron Howard
Kate Hudson
Felicity Huffman
William Hurt
Samuel L. Jackson
Angelina Jolie
James Earl Jones
Tommy Lee Jones
Catherine Zeta-Jones
Milla Jovovich
Lawrence Kasdan
Phillip Kaufman
Diane Keaton
Kevin Klein
Keira Knightley
Martin Kove
Diane Ladd

Nearly Famous

Martin Landau
Jessica Lange
Diane Lane
John Lasseter
Queen Latifah
Martin Lawrence
Heath Ledger
Brandon Lee
Spike Lee
Jennifer Jason Leigh
Jack Lemmon
Barry Levinson
Juliette Lewis
Ray Liotta
Lucy Liu
Lindsey Lohan
Jon Lovitz
Jennifer Lopez
Shirley MacLaine
James Mangold
Michael Mann
Joe Mantegna
Toby Maquire
Barry Marshall
Garry Marshall
Penny Marshall
Melissa Mathison
Steve Martin
Andie MacDowell
Matthew McConaughey
Mary McDonnell
Elizabeth McGovern
Ewan McGregor
Nancy Meyers
Sienna Miller
Liza Minnelli
Alfred Molina

Demi Moore
Dudley Moore
Julianne Moore
Viggo Mortensen
Paul Newman
Mike Nichols
Nick Nolte
Edward Norton
Chuck Norris
Clive Owen
Al Pacino
Brian Palma
Bill Paxton
Amanda Peet
Joe Pesci
Wolfgang Petersen
William Peterson
Michelle Pfeiffer
Joaquin Phoenix
Joe Piscopo
Brad Pitt
Oliver Platt
Anna Popplewell
Kelly Preston
Vincent Price
Dennis Quaid
Sam Raimi
Robert Redford
Keanu Reeves
Ivan Reitman
Burt Reynolds
Debbie Reynolds
Kevin Reynolds
Giovanni Ribisi
Denise Richards
Joely Richardson
Natasha Richardson

Reba Merrill

Alan Rickman
Julia Roberts
Tim Robbins
Chris Rock
Gary Ross
Gena Rowlands
Kurt Russell
Rene Russo
Meg Ryan
Winona Ryder
Gene Sacks
Eva Marie Saint
Peter Sarsgaard
Adam Sandler
John Sanford
Greta Scacchi
Jack Scalia
Volker Schlöndorff
Rob Schneider
Barbet Schroeder
Arnold Schwarzenegger
Robert Schwentke
Martin Scorsese
Ridley Scott
Seann William Scott
Tony Scott
Kyra Sedgwick
Omar Sharif
Charlie Sheen
Martin Sheen
Brooke Shields
Joel Schumacher
M. Night Shyamalan
Jonathan Silverman
Sinbad
Gary Sinise
Christian Slater
Glenn Slater
Will Smith
Wesley Snipes
Brittany Snow
Stephen Soderberg
Mira Sorveno
Sissy Spacek
David Spade
Tori Spelling
Jerry Springer
Nick Stahl
Terrence Stamp
Jimmy Stewart
Jon Stewart
Ben Stiller
Sting
Eric Stoltz
Oliver Stone
Sharon Stone
Madeleine Stowe
Meryl Streep
Hillary Swank
Tilda Swinton
Max Thieriot
Emma Thompson
Betty Thomas
Kristin Scott Thomas
Billy Bob Thornton
Uma Therman
Charlize Theron
Meg Tilly
Marisa Tomei
Lilly Tomlin
Stanley Tong
Michelle Trachtenberg
John Travolta
Randy Travis

Kathleen Turner
Jon Turteltaub
Liv Tyler
Brenda Vaccaro
Gore Verbinski
Paul Verhoeven
Jon Voight
Christopher Walken
Paul Walker
Dee Wallace
Lesley Ann Warren
Mark Waters
Denzel Washington
Sigourney Weaver
Rachel Weisz
Raquel Welch
Forest Whitaker
Robin Williams
Treat Williams
The Rock
Bruce Willis
Luke Wilson
Owen Wilson
Rita Wilson
Debra Winger
Reese Witherspoon
Simon Wincer
Stan Winston
Robert Wise
Scott Wolf
John Woo
James Woods
Morgan York
Steve Zahn
Renee Zellweger

About the Author

Reba Merrill is an international entertainment journalist and an Emmy Award-wining producer and Cable ACE nominee. She has interviewed nearly everyone from legendary movie stars to Hollywood's hot new celebrities and the silver screen's biggest box-office draws in over 500 films. Some of her favorite interviews include: Julia Roberts, Al Pacino, Robin Williams, Dustin Hoffman, Harrison Ford, Denzel Washington, Jack Lemmon, Jimmy Stewart, Meryl Streep, Cher and Whitney Houston.

Reba hosted four talk shows: *REBA* and *Good Morning Arizona*, ABC in Phoenix and *Sun Up San Diego,* CBS and Cox Cable's *That's Life* which earned her an Emmy Award as well as a Cable ACE nomination.

For over 20 years, Reba's in-depth interviews with the stars about their careers, fears, hopes and dreams have become TV specials, electronic press kits and celebrity profiles, now seen worldwide. Based on this body of work, Reba was elected to the Academy of Motion Pictures Arts and Sciences and more recently, The British Academy of Film and Television Arts/LA (BAFTA). She has been a working member of AFTRA since 1969 as well as a member of the Publicists Guild since 1984.

She lives in Marina Del Rey, California with her husband.

Ginny Weissman is an Emmy-nominated writer, producer and director as well as a journalist, author, manager and publisher. Ginny's acclaimed documentaries have appeared on A&E, The History Channel, Discovery Health Channel and PBS. Ginny began her career as a journalist at *The Chicago Tribune* as the editor of TV Week magazine where she interviewed hundreds of celebrities and wrote personality profiles. She is the co-author of two critically acclaimed, best-selling books, *The Dick Van Dyke Show, Anatomy of a Classic* and *Champagne Music, The Lawrence Welk Show* (St. Martin's Press). She lives in Palm Springs, California.

CPSIA information can be obtained at www.ICGtesting.com
Printed in the USA
LVOW070257280512

283526LV00011B/131/P